STUDIES IN ENGLISH LITERATURE

Volume XXXV

Clyomon

and

Clamydes

A Critical Edition

by

BETTY J. LITTLETON
Stephens College, Columbia, Missouri

1968
MOUTON
THE HAGUE · PARIS

Printed in The Netherlands by Mouton & Co., Printers, The Hague.

ACKNOWLEDGEMENTS

I should like to express my thanks to those who generously offered their help with various parts of this edition, particularly to Richard Hosley and Edwin Miller and to the staffs of the University of Missouri Library and the Stephens College Library.

I am indebted to the Henry E. Huntington Library for permission to use the facsimile of the *Clyomon and Clamydes* title page and to the Harvard University Press for permission to quote the lyric "No pleasure without some paine" from Hyder E. Rollins' edition of *The Paradise of Dainty Devices* (1927).

CONTENTS

Acknowledgements 5

Abbreviations. 9

Introduction 11

1. The Text of This Edition 13
   a. *The Printing* 14
   b. *The Copy* 16
   c. *This Edition* 19

2. Authorship 22
   a. *Ascriptions* 22
   b. *Clyomon and Clamydes* and *Common Conditions* 23

3. Date 30

4. Staging and Production 34

5. Sources 38
   a. *Perceforest* 38
   b. *The Morality Play* 49

6. *Clyomon and Clamydes:* An Early Romantic Play . . 53
   a. *The Early Romantic Drama* 53
   b. *Style* 55
   c. *Significance* 63

Clyomon and Clamydes 67

Notes 157

Appendix A: Emendations of Accidentals 186

Appendix B: The Romantic Play 1570–1585 195

Appendix C: "No Pleasure Without Some Paine" . . . 199

ABBREVIATIONS

Abbott	E. A. Abbott, *A Shakespearian Grammar* (London, 1901).
Apius and Virginia	R(ichard) B(ower), *Apius and Virginia* (Malone Society Reprint, 1911).
Bullen	*The Works of George Peele*, ed. A. H. Bullen (London, 1888).
Chambers	E. K. Chambers, *The Elizabethan Stage* (Oxford, 1923).
Conditions	*Common Conditions*, ed. Tucker Brooke (New Haven, 1915).
Cunliffe	*Early English Classical Tragedies*, ed. John W. Cunliffe (Oxford, 1912).
Damon and Pithias	Richard Edwards, *Damon and Pithias* (Malone Society Reprint, 1957).
Dodsley	*A Select Collection of Old English Plays*, compiled by Robert Dodsley, ed. W. Carew Hazlitt (London, 1874).
Dyce	*The Works of George Peele*, ed. Alexander Dyce (London, 1829 and 1839).
Faerie Queene	Edmund Spenser, *The Faerie Queene*, ed. J. C. Smith and E. de Selincourt in *The Poetical Works* (Oxford, 1952).
Forsythe	R. W. Forsythe, *The Relation of Shirley's Plays to the Elizabethan Drama* (New York, 1914).
Freeburg	Victor O. Freeburg, *Disguise Plots in Elizabethan Drama* (New York, 1915).

Grissell	John Phillip, *The Play of the Patient Grissell* (Malone Society Reprint, 1909).
Lods	Jeanne Lods, *Le Roman de Perceforest. Origines – Composition – Characters – Valeur et Influence* (Geneva, 1951).
Looking Glass	*A Looking Glass for London and England* (Malone Society Reprint, 1932).
O.E.D.	*The Oxford English Dictionary*, 1884–1928.
Old Wives	George Peele, *Old Wives Tale* (Malone Society Reprint, 1909).
Partridge	Eric Partridge, *Shakespeare's Bawdy* (London, 1955).
Puttenham	George Puttenham, *The Arte of English Poesie*, ed. Edward Arbor (Birmingham, 1869).
Respublica	*Respublica*, ed. Leonard A. Magnus (Early English Text Society, 1905), vol. 94, Extra Series.
Selimus	*The Tragical Reign of Selimus* (1594) (Malone Society Reprint, 1908).
Tilley	M. P. Tilley, *A Dictionary of the Proverbs in England in the Sixteenth and Seventeenth Centuries* (Ann Arbor, Michigan, 1950).
True Tragedie	*The True Tragedie of Richard the Third* (Malone Society Reprint, 1929).
Whiting	B. J. Whiting, *Proverbs in the Earlier English Drama* (Cambridge, 1939).
Wyld	Henry Cecil Wyld, *A History of Modern Colloquial English* (New York, 1920).

The customary abbreviations are used for periodicals.

INTRODUCTION

While the considerable vogue of the romantic drama between 1570 and 1585 is well attested by the Revels Accounts for those years and by other contemporary records and literary allusions,[1] our understanding of the nature of this drama – its aesthetic, its purpose, its structure and language, manner of staging and the like – remains somewhat imprecise. The reason, of course, is paucity of factual evidence. Of the thirty play titles from this period which clearly denote romantic material, only three plays – *Clyomon and Clamydes* (1576), *Common Conditions* (S. R. 1576) and *The Rare Triumphs of Love and Fortune* (1582) – have come down to us. And while the Revels Accounts, for instance, are copious in their suggestions about the elaborate staging of the early romantic plays, these suggestions do little to modify the vagueness of our understanding of a genre which is separated from us in time and taste by so many generations. Hence the only road back begins with the three plays themselves – with attempts to identify their similarities and to isolate their distinguishing features. Tucker Brooke, in writing about the authorship of *Common Conditions*, stated the problem some years ago when he concluded that the drama of the period

... is not copiously enough represented to permit of positive distinction between the peculiarities of a single author and the characteristics of a school. Many similarities which at first suggest common authorship may have been the universal property of the writers of the period.... Whether these similarities ... justify the assumption of common authorship ... can only be fairly determined, I think, when

[1] See Appendix B.

we are more in a position than at present to estimate how far such devices belonged to the general repertory of dramatic writers at the time the plays were produced.[2]

Though Brooke's concern was with a specific authorship problem, his statement and the method it implies can be extended to include most of the details relevant to our knowledge of this drama. Only when we are in a position to establish or dis-establish authorship claims for *Clyomon and Clamydes, Common Conditions* and *Love and Fortune*, only when we are able to date them, examine their use of source-material, infer their methods of staging and acting from what has been termed their "theatrical physiognomy",[3] and assess their aesthetic principles as they are revealed in dramaturgical technique – only when we are able to work through these problems will we be able to make a "distinction between the peculiarities of a single author and the characteristics of a school" and hence to isolate those devices that "belonged to the general repertory of dramatic writers at the time the plays were produced". Though many of its conclusions are necessarily limited, it is in this larger context that the present edition has its relevance.

---

[2] *Common Conditions*, Tucker Brooke (ed.) (New Haven, 1915), p. 84.
[3] Rudolph Stamm, "Elizabethan Stage-Practice and the Transmutation of Source Material by the Dramatists", *ShS*, XII (1959), 60-64.

1

THE TEXT OF THIS EDITION

Though it is by now an irrefutable principle that establishment of authoritative texts should precede literary analysis and, in the case of our early drama, that bibliographical and textual analysis should precede extra-literary analysis (i.e. questions of date, authorship, sources) as well as literary analysis, the truth of this truism is particularly apparent in the case of *Clyomon and Clamydes*. To anticipate somewhat, the question of authorship, for example, is largely dependent on a study of linguistic preferences that might have originated at any one of several stages in the transmission of the text – with author, scribe, bookkeeper, or compositor. Bibliographical analysis alone provides a thread out of this minor literary labyrinth; and though it cannot provide a basis for saying who the author *was*, it can provide a basis for saying rather emphatically who he was *not*. In a similar fashion, the establishment of a limiting backward date is entirely dependent on inferences that may be drawn from the text about the staging of the play, a process complicated by an apparently composite text reflecting a bookkeeper's annotations and alterations through its first forty-nine pages and then, rather abruptly, at its fiftieth page (sig. G3v) and continuing through its final thirteen pages, reflecting an authorial manuscript. Clearly, even the most tentative conclusions about the staging of the play – and, in turn, its date – are dependent on textual and bibliographical analysis. In the problem of dating, in fact, *Clyomon and Clamydes* illustrates how the problems of an early text mesh – how their solutions are interdependent and hence must be held in suspension until all of the available facts and inferences have been marshalled; for in the case of *Clyomon and Clamydes*, the anomolous and often contradictory implications about staging coincide with – and to an extent are identical with – textual anomolies and confusions that divide the quarto at sig. G3v. But the evidence – for provenance of the text, authorship, date and staging – is mutually supporting. Let us take them in an order which should be imagined as simultaneous but which must be sorted out singly for our better understanding.

a. *The Printing*

The only authoritative text of *Clyomon and Clamydes* (Greg, Bibliography, no. 157) [1] is the quarto printed by Thomas Creede in 1599. The play undoubtedly belongs to an earlier time, however; the title-page ascription to the Queen's Men would date it sometime between 1583 and 1593/4, and it is probable that it was acted even earlier.[2] It was not entered in The Stationers' Register, but since Creede entered four other Queen's plays and printed a fifth in 1594, we can assume that he probably acquired *Clyomon and Clamydes* in the same year. We do not know, of course, why he delayed publication until 1599. (He printed *A Looking Glass for London and England, The True Tragedy of Richard the Third* and *Selimus*, the unregistered play, in 1594 and *The Famous Victories of Henry the Fifth* and *The Scottish History of James the Fourth* in 1598.) [3] But it is possible that its publication that year reflects not delay but opportunism of the kind that was to bring forth old plays like *Mucedorus* (revived 1607) in an attempt to satisfy changing audience tastes. At any rate, Creede's 1599 quarto stands as a curious example of the resurrection of a literary taste that had seen its heyday some twenty years earlier; and though its bibliographical skeleton suggests revision for public theater production, reasons for revision can only be inferred from other, collateral evidence.

Both the composition and presswork indicate an unusual but definite order in the production of the quarto. Although the first

---

[1] Collation: 4°, A-H4 I2, 34 leaves unnumbered; A1-1v blank; A2 TP: A2v Prologue; A3 Text; I1v finis; I2-2v blank.
[2] See Introduction, pp. 30-33.
[3] Chambers, III, 184n.

two sheets appear to be the work of a single compositor (A), sheet C introduces the work of a second man (B) who continues to collaborate on the composition throughout the remainder of the text. On the basis of distinguishing spelling and typographical characteristics it is possible to assign with some certainty all but three of the quarto's type-pages, and although the three remaining pages – E3, E3v and G2v – contain conflicting evidence, one may conjecture their assignment to Compositor B on the basis of their position. The pattern that emerges indicates a somewhat unusual scheme of collaboration beginning with sheet C. Rather than divide their work by inner and outer formes, the normal practice in Elizabethan printing of quartos, they divided each forme, with the result that each compositor was responsible for four consecutive pages in sheets C-F:

> A: C-C2v, D-D2v, E-E2v and E4v, F3-F4v
> B: C3-C4v, D3-D4v, E3-4, F-F2v

The only exception to the pattern occurs in E(o) where Compositor A set E4v. Although sheets G and H continue the collaboration, the division of work is no longer equal; here Compositor A set 10 pages to B's 6 – all of G and H(o) and sig. 3 of sheets G and H(i). Each compositor set one page of half-sheet I(i).

Printing was performed with two skeleton formes – I for the outer and II for the inner formes of sheets A and B. Though a new skeleton (III) replaces I at the inner forme of sheet C, it continues to alternate regularly with the other skeleton through F(i). After that point, however, the regular order of the skeletons gives way so that the printing of G(i) precedes F(o), G(o) and H(o) in that order, and halfsheet I(i) precedes H(i). Or, since there is a possibility that two presses were used from sheet C onward, one press may have printed the formes set with skeleton II – C(o), D(i), E(i), F(o), F(i), H(o) and H(i) – while the second press alternated with it, printing formes set with skeleton III – C(i), D(o), E(o), G(o), G(i) and I(i). In either event, the regularity of the printing process (from outer to inner forme) is interrupted after the printing of F(i), with the result that one forme of sheet G precedes F(o).

The simultaneous departures from the patterned order of both composition and press-work after F(i) is, of course, indication either of some difficulty in the print shop – possibly incompetence on the part of Compositor B – or of irregularity in the copy that made the departures from the normal pattern necessary if the composition was to keep pace with the press work.

The first charge is unlikely since Creede's compositors during this time are known to have been unusually careful, accurate, and faithful to their original – at least in the case of dramatic prints; and compositor B is known to have been even more careful and conservative in his treatment of copy than compositor A.[4] Instead, the sudden diminution of Compositor B's output in the last two and one-half sheets (7 pages to compositor A's 11) lends support to the inference that some alteration in the copy made the composition of sheets G and H sufficiently difficult to prevent him from keeping pace with his fellow worker. The early imposition of the half-sheet – although the practice was not uncommon in Creede's shop (e.g. *Menechmi* Q1 and *Romeo and Juliet* Q2) – also probably reflects the need to re-adjust the time of composition so that it would be in balance with the schedule of presswork.

b. *The Copy*

Evidence of alteration in the copy at the point of interruption and irregularity in the composition and presswork at G(i) – specifically at G3v – is abundant. Up to that point the text is consistent, accurate, and relatively free from error; and it shows clear signs of alteration, addition, and correction for production purposes. To what is clearly an authorial direction – *"Here let them make a noyse as though they were Marriners. And after* Clyomon *Knight of G. S. come in with one."* – an annotator, presumably the book-

---

[4] A comparison of the composition and press-work of the 11 dramatic prints from manuscript copy and 6 reprints that Creede produced between 1594 and 1606 indicates that both the original compositor and then his helper, whose work appears from 1598 onward, were careful and accurate and that they were unusually faithful to the original in both substantives and accidentals – Compositor B somewhat more so than Compositor A. George Walton Williams, "The Good Quarto of *Romeo and Juliet*" (unpublished Ph.D. dissertation, University of Virginia, Charlottesville, 1957).

keeper, has added the direction *"Enter* Clyomon, *Boateswaine"*. (A similar duplication occurs at ll. 273 and 282-3.) Other indications of the bookkeeper's hand are the abundant directions in these pages for props, special theatrical effects (e.g. the descent and ascent of Providence), sound effects (e.g. *"Sing here"* or *"Sound here once"* and *"Sound second time"*), and even a dog.[5] At sig. G3v, however, a change in the usual speech prefix for Alexander the Great from *Alexander* to *King* signals a spate of inconsistencies, errors and confusions that characterize the text from this point on. The Vice, who has been designated *Shift* or *Subtle Shift* throughout, becomes *Knowledge, Shift* and *The Vice*; and the heroine Neronis is designated variously as *Neronis, Page* and *Curdaser*. Four other speech prefixes are mis-assigned and three are omitted in this portion of the text (compared with four such errors in all before sig. G3v). Directions for entrances are omitted six times, lines needed to complete couplets are omitted at least five times, one line is unfinished (l. 2116), and a half-line belonging to Clyomon – *"Say on your mind"* – is printed in italics and inserted at the beginning of a complete line which is assigned to Neronis. (The inference is that the words were added in the margin without a prefix.) And finally, the last 13 pages contain 66 lines of eight-foot iambic couplets (ll. 2148-2214) – the only extended departure from the regular fourteener measure of the play.

Two hypotheses may be formulated to account for these anomolies that divide the text before and after sig. G3v: one postulates composite copy (a prompt book supplemented by foul papers) and the other postulates partial revision (annotated foul papers). The two duplicated stage directions in conjunction with some fifteen other stage directions (all before sig. G3v) of the "permissive", "indefinite", and "descriptive" variety that Greg says are normally authorial [6] would ordinarily argue for the theory of an-

---

[5] An author presumably would not require an animal unless he was writing for a definite troupe which would have the trained animal available. Hence "it is possible that some of the animal acts preserved in printed stage plays are the result of the printers' use of acting versions with interpolated matter". Louis B. Wright, "Animal Actors on the English Stage Before 1642", *PMLA*, XLII (1927), 699.

[6] W. W. Greg, *The Shakespeare First Folio* (Oxford, 1955), p. 138.

notation and revision on an authorial manuscript. Yet such directions were occasionally retained in the prompt book (as in the case of *Edmund Ironsides*, ll. 733-915, for example) and even in the purely theatrical plots and hence are not infallible signs of an authorial manuscript.[7] A theory of revision, moreover, cannot account for the distinctive scribal characteristics that divide the two portions of the text. These point, instead, to two manuscripts and hence to two different kinds of copy.

Certain phonetic spellings in the first portion, for example, suggest that these pages are the work of a scribe who had heard the words pronounced but who gave no attention to accuracy (in the case of *Serbarus*, l. 62) or even to their meaning (in the case of *Cur Daceer*, ll. 1639 and 1640). An extended confusion in speech prefixes at ll. 595-605 also suggests the work of a playhouse scribe since it reflects the usual practice of writing a full page of dialogue in the prompt book and then filling in the names in the ruled-off, left-hand margin (a practice that "tended to produce bad alignment").[8] A theory of revision also fails to account for the abrupt alteration in punctuation and spelling after sig. G3 – in the use of the colon to close speeches when the end of a speech coincides with the first line of a couplet (37 times in 13 pages as compared with 15 times in 50 pages) and in the introduction of certain spellings (e.g. *Nerones, Cliomon* and *Cœur d'acer*) that do not occur in the earlier portion of the text. Hence the best explanation for such divergencies in purely mechanical details of the copy is a theory of composite copy – that is, two distinct manuscripts, one emanating from the playhouse and the other from the author, one a prompt book and the other foul papers.[9]

---

[7] W. W. Greg, *Dramatic Documents from the Elizabethan Playhouses* (Oxford, 1931), I, 208.

[8] W. W. Greg, *The Editorial Problem in Shakespeare* (Oxford, 1951), p. 34.

[9] Collateral evidence for an authorial manuscript behind the final pages of the text lies in a double reference to a scene that has been cut from the earlier part of the play. In the final scene Neronis drops her disguise and confronts Clyomon, her lover, who still does not recognize her, and she re-traces the major scenes in which she and Clyomon have figured in

c. *This Edition*

After its publication in 1599, except for occasional mention in
seventeenth- and eighteenth-century play-lists, *Clyomon and Cla-*
mydes received no attention until Dyce included it in his modern-
spelling edition of Peele's works in 1839. This edition was followed by Bullen's edition of 1888, also in a collection of Peele's
work even though Bullen doubted Peele's authorship. Subsequently the play was issued in type facsimile by the Malone Society
in 1913 and, in the same year, in photographic facsimile in J. S.
Farmer's *Student Facsimile Texts.*

The present edition is based on a collation of the six extant
exemplars of the 1599 quarto and on a collation of this "copy-
text" with the two nineteenth-century editions. A collation of the
six copies of the 1599 quarto revealed six press variants.[10]

Since the quarto is best described as a faithful setting by

---

an effort to force his recognition. Thus she tells how she found him on the
shore of her father's kingdom and nursed him back to health, how they
plighted their faith, how Clyomon left to pursue his enemy and Neronis
was kidnapped during his absence, how Clyomon pursued the kidnapper
and killed him, and finally, how Clyomon took into his service a page
(Neronis in disguise). All of these scenes occur in the play; but Neronis
alludes to one further scene which does not occur:
In Forrest once, who gave you drink, whereas you stood with sword
in hand,
Fearing least some had you pursude for sleying of your enemie?
Ten lines later she refers to the scene again:
I gave you drinke in Forrest sure, when you with drought were like
to die.
Since the episode appears neither in the source nor in the play, the double
reference here suggests that it was an invention of the playwright's that
was cut during revision and preparation of the manuscript for production.
The "Tyger fell" of l. 97 may also be evidence for cutting. It appears that
the playwright condenses three episodes from *Perceforest* – Lyonnel du
Glar's conquest of the two lions, the flying serpent and the Giant with the
Golden Hair – into the single quest of the flying serpent. But the reference
to the "Tyger fell" may indicate his original use of two episodes rather
than one from the source.
[10] Copies collated (all extant): B (British Museum); F (Folger Shakespeare
Library); H (Henry E. Huntington Library); J (Heber-Huth-Jones copy
now owned by Louis B. Silver); P (Pforzheimer Library); W (White copy

Creede's compositors A and B of the prompt copy supplemented by the unknown playwright's foul papers and hence probably reflects his intentions with reasonable accuracy, I have edited lightly and conservatively. That is, in both accidentals and substantives, I have made alterations only in cases of clear press mistakes and equally clear textual corruption, and I have followed the same principle in the adoption or rejection of emendations made by earlier editors. (I have not seen fit to include the results of the historical collation – except to record Dyce's or Bullen's readings when I have adopted them or, in some cases, when I have rejected a reading that nevertheless has something to recommend it.) Substantive emendations are given at the bottom of each page and emendations of accidentals are given in Appendix A.

In spelling, I have followed the copy-text except for silent alteration of speech prefixes to make them consistent. I have changed punctuation when the copy-text reproduced what are probably compositors' errors or when the punctuation, by the standard of the text itself, is inconsistent – for example, when a full stop is omitted at the end of a speech. Changes in spelling and punctuation are listed among the emendations of accidentals. Similarly, when I have introduced changes in the typography of the copy-text – in the italicizing of proper names in the text, or the change of italicized names to roman – these are also listed among the alterations of accidentals.

Silent alterations for which no notes are given include the regular expansion of speech prefixes and the normalizing of their spelling, the alteration of the typography of stage directions to make them consistent with the normal printing practice of the compositors, the expansion of abbreviations, the capitalization of lower-case letters after full stops (excepting queries), and the

at Harvard University Library). The variants, all in accidentals, occurred on the following pages: sig. B1v, l. 178 ring,] ring. (Corrected: B, P, W. H; Uncorrected: F, J); sig. C3v, l. 627 jolt-headed] jolt headed (Corrected: B, F; Uncorrected (?): H, J, P, W); sig. D1v, l. 746 wonne.] wonne, (Corrected: B, F, J, P, W; Uncorrected: H); sig. E4v, l. 1254 mans apparell] mans-apparell (Corrected: F; Uncorrected: B, H, J, P, W); sig. F4v, l. 1566 praise,] praise. (Corrected: F, H, J, W; Uncorrected: B, P); sig. H1v, l. 1921 hest] heft (Corrected: H, W, F, J; Uncorrected (?): B, P).

correction of wrong-font letters. Typographical features such as the long *s* and the use of *i* for *j*, medial *u* for *v*, and initial *v* for *u* have been modernized. In line numbering and scene division I have followed the Malone Society Reprint.[11]

[11] In its mechanics the editorial method is modelled on Fredson Bowers' method as outlined in *The Dramatic Works of Thomas Dekker* (Cambridge, 1953), I, xv-xviii. In the Presentation of emendations and collations, I have used the symbols advocated by R. B. McKerrow in *Prolegomena for the Oxford Shakespeare* (Oxford, 1939).

2

AUTHORSHIP

a. *Ascriptions*

In spite of various attempts to assign the authorship of *Clyomon and Clamydes* to one or another of the minor dramatists of the '70's and '80's, the play is – and is likely to remain – anonymous. The initial ascription came from Dyce, whose discovery of a copy of the play with "a MS. note in a very old hand" attributing it to George Peele prompted him to undertake an edition of the play which he added, in 1839, to the two-volume edition of Peele's works he had published ten years earlier. The copy in question has since been lost, but Dyce's integrity as an editor lent considerable strength to the ascription [1] so that, although Peele's next editor, Bullen, questioned it in the introduction to his edition in 1888 and suggested, instead, Richard Edwards, it was not until 1889-90 in a scholarly exchange between two German students that Peele's authorship was finally discredited.[2]

[1] The ascription to Peele was accepted by Ward, Minto, Symonds, Lammerhirt. It was called into question in 1869 (T. Corser, *Collectanea Anglo Poetica*, Part IV [1869], 407). It has been twice suggested that the manuscript note on which Dyce based his ascription may have been a modern forgery. See A. Brandl, *Quellen des Weltlichen Dramas in England vor Shakespeare*, Vol. LXXX in *Quellen und Forschungen*, ed. A. Brandl (Strassburg, 1898), cxii; E. H. C. Oliphant, "Problems of Authorship in Elizabethan Drama", *MP*, VIII (1911), 432.

[2] See for example T. Larsen, "The Canon of Peele's Works", *MP*, XVII (1928), 191-199; Harold M. Dowling, "The Date and Order of Peele's Plays", *N&Q*, 164 (1933), 183-185; David Horne, *The Life and Minor Works of George Peele* (New Haven, 1952), pp. 65-109. The 1889-90 exchange was begun by Leon Kellner, who argues that unless the play is a parody of the popular romantic drama of the time, Peele had nothing to

Immediate suggestions came from Fleay, who attributed the play to Robert Wilson and later to R[ichard] B[ower], to whom he also attributed *Common Conditions*,[3] and from Kittredge, who ascribed it to Thomas Preston.[4] In both cases, however, the ascriptions were of doubtful use since they were made to men whose very identity is uncertain [5] and they were based on verbal and technical similarities (e.g. use of personifications, a roguish Vice, classical allusions) that are difficult if not impossible to interpret with any degree of accuracy.

b. *Clyomon and Clamydes* and *Common Conditions*

In his edition of *Common Conditions* in 1916, Tucker Brooke tentatively suggested that *Conditions* and *Clyomon* might be by

---

do with it. He notes in defense of his thesis that the play contains word forms, grammatical constructions and vocabulary that do not appear in Peele's works and metrical patterns and abundant alliterative lines which are not characteristic of him. He believes that the rhetorical excesses of *Clyomon* have no parallel in Peele's known works, and he points to the absence in *Clyomon* of the unifying theme and interest in characterization that distinguish Peele's work. Leon Kellner, "*Sir Clyomon and Sir Clamydes*. Ein romantisches Schauspiel des 16. Jahrhunderts", *Englische Studien*, XIII (1889), 187-229. Kellner's study was answered the next year by Rudolph Fischer, who suggests, quite rightly, that Kellner's argument is essentially that Peele could not have written so bad a play. Fischer's view is that the young, immature Peele could and probably did write it. He shows that Kellner's study of the language failed to take into account textual corruptions, the playwright's predilection for eye-rimes and the use of rustic dialect which account for most of the unusual words in the text. He believes that the grammatical constructions, metrical patterns and alliterative lines which Kellner attacks are in fact devices employed unsuccessfully by an immature poet. He points out that the plot and construction of the play show an orderliness and symmetry which Kellner overlooks and suggests that Peele borrowed both the balanced construction and the bombastic rhetoric of the set speeches from renaissance classical drama. Rudolph Fischer, "Zur Frage nach der Autorschaft von *Sir Clyomon und Sir Clamides*", *Englische Studien*, XIV (1890), 344-365.
[3] Frederick Gard Fleay, *A Biographical Chronicle of the English Drama* (London, 1891), II, 296.
[4] G. L. Kittredge, "Notes on Elizabethan Plays", *JEGP*, II (1898), 8-9.
[5] The R.B. of *Apius and Virginia* has not yet been satisfactorily identified, and the Thomas Preston of *Cambises* may or may not be the Thomas Preston (1537) who rose to the position of vice-chancellor of Cambridge and was the author of at least three anti-papal ballads.

the same anonymous author (though not the R. B. of *Apius and Virginia*, as Fleay had suggested earlier).[6] He pointed out similarities in style, structure, and motif and several instances of parallel (or almost parallel) passages that are indeed compelling if not convincing arguments for their common authorship. There is, for example, their rhetorical style, which is characterized by allusion, repetition, rhetorical question, ornamental adjectives (e.g. *wearied toile, painfull travail*), infinitive constructions (e.g. *for to speake, for to perswade*) and ornate constructions like the repetition of a pronoun after a substantive (e.g. *dame Tellus shee, queene Flora shee, Cardolus hee*). Both plays employ certain characteristic constructions – mainly *for why, whereas* (where) and *if case* – and word forms like *vade, denay, frustrate* (adj.), *pretend* (intend), *neare* (nearer) and so on. Similar motifs appear in each play – a hero frees captives who have been imprisoned in the villain's (Bryan's, Cardolus') castle; the Vice assumes one or more pseudonyms, is involved in the double love-plot and, prompted by cowardice, joins forces with the villain of the piece; a lady confesses her love via the conventional image of the storm-tossed ship; mariners enter from their cock-boat.[7] And finally, the plays have passages which are roughly parallel: the rhetorical "farewell" speeches of both Lamphedon and Sedmond in *Common Conditions* and of Clamydes;[8] the image of the storm-tossed ship used by Sabia in *Common Conditions* and by both Clamydes and Neronis in *Clyomon and Clamydes*;[9] and the speeches in which Lamphedon and Neronis contemplate suicide.[10]

Yet in spite of similarities in vocabulary, style, and motifs, these plays reveal differences which argue against their common authorship and suggest instead that their similarities reflect the vogue of a particular poetic and dramatic idiom which characterized the romantic drama of the 1570's and '80's. In any event it must be admitted that arguments either for or against their common

[6] For similarities in diction, see the notes of this edition and Tucker Brooke's edition of *Common Conditions, op. cit.*
[7] Tucker Brooke, *op. cit.*, pp. xiv and 84-85.
[8] *Conditions*, ll. 468-477; *Clyomon*, ll. 882-889.
[9] *Conditions*, ll. 840-850; *Clyomon*, ll. 1-32; 1055-1068.
[10] *Conditions*, ll. 1515-1523; *Clyomon*, ll. 1535-1548.

authorship are precarious, for the usual tests based on internal evidence – stylistic correspondences (rhetoric, metrics, imagery, parallel passages), literary correspondences (theme, characterization, dramatic technique) and linguistic correspondences (e.g. distinctive grammatical forms such as verb endings, pronoun forms, contractions, and the like) – cannot be supplemented by any other known works by the presumed author or authors of the two plays.[11] Thus it is only possible to suggest that certain differences between them probably point to two different authors.

Objective linguistic evidence, for instance, argues strongly against their common authorship.[12] Most significant are the characteristic interjections which differentiate the two plays. *Conditions* is characterized by the form *Ha* (it appears 75 times, in contrast to *Ah* or *A*, which appears 25 times). This interjection does not appear in *Clyomon*, which is characterized instead by a marked preference for sentences beginning with *well*; and the word appears so often – 64 times at the beginning of speeches alone – that it may be considered an habitual mannerism. Speeches opening with *well* occur only 18 times in *Conditions*.

There are also differences in diction. *Conditions* is characterized by certain contractions – *tis* (8), *wonnot* (3), *twas* (2), and

---

[11] The use of internal evidence in authorship problems has been reviewed recently in a series of articles, "The Case for Internal Evidence", published in volumes 61-64 of the *Bulletin of the New York Public Library*. For the particular problems involved in the interpretation of internal evidence in Elizabethan plays see M. St. C. Byrne, "Bibliographical Clues in Collaborate Plays", *The Library*, Fourth Series, XIII (1932-3), 21-48; S. Schoenbaum, "Internal Evidence and the Attribution of Elizabethan Plays", *BNYPL*, LXV (1961), 102-124 and *Internal Evidence and Elizabethan Dramatic Authorship* (Evanston, Illinois, 1966), pp. 147-219.

[12] The most objective authorship tests to date have been devised by Cyrus Hoy in his work on the Beaumont and Fletcher canon. The tests are based on linguistic, stylistic and verbal criteria of an objective nature which distinguish the preferences of individual authors – e.g. Fletcher's preference for *ye* rather than *you*, for certain contractions (*'em, i'th, o'th, h'as*), Middleton's preference for *a'th* rather than *o'th* and for *a*, which he uses for *of* and *on*, and distinctive stylistic preferences (e.g. placement of the caesura, use of feminine endings, syntax, characteristic interjections, preference for nouns in the vocative, and the like). See Cyrus Hoy, "The Shares of Fletcher and His Collaborators in the Beaumont and Fletcher Canon", Parts I-VII, *SB*, VIII (1956)-XV (1962).

minks (methinks) (2) – which do not appear in *Clyomon*; and *Clyomon* is peculiarly characterized by the contraction in the phrase *ant shall please*, which occurs 23 times in that play and does not occur in *Conditions*. *Conditions* is characterized also by the use of *iwis* (4), by the repeated use of *seem* in the sense of "think fit" or "attempt", and by the verb *to fine* – "else had I finde my dayes", "when death shall finde thy dayes", and "thy vitall dayes to fine". These words do not occur in *Clyomon*, which is characterized instead by words with unusual prefixes: *perstand*, *prepare* (repair), *pretend* (intend), *prevail* (avail) and the like. (*Pretend* in the sense of "intend" also occurs in *Conditions*, l. 106.)

While linguistic evidence is not conclusive, its suggestion of distinct authorship for the two plays is corroborated by other evidence based on style and literary criteria. For one thing, the metrical regularity of *Conditions* is much less striking than that of *Clyomon*, particularly in passages of dialogue, where the author of *Conditions* tends to break away from the fourteener and from the iambic pattern in general. *Conditions*, moreover, is characterized by occasional passages of poulter's measure (e.g. ll. 470-75, 484-87) – a form which does not appear among the metrical variants of *Clyomon*. And *Clyomon* is characterized by occasional use of eight-foot iambic couplets, a form which does not appear in *Conditions*.[13] There is also a distinct difference in the employment of feminine endings, for *Conditions* alters the regular masculine ending of the fourteener only six times, while *Clyomon* alters it some 30 times.

The number of classical allusions in *Common Conditions* more than doubles the number in *Clyomon and Clamydes*, and they are perhaps slightly less conventional than the repeated references in *Clyomon* to Mars, Venus, and the Fates. Proverbial material also throws doubt on the probability that a consistent technique connects the two plays, for while Conditions is given the typical Vice's spread of proverbs – a total of 28 – Shift is given only eight.[14]

[13]   ll. 372-3, 413-4, 492-3, 2148-2214.
[14]   B. J. Whiting's conclusion about the common authorship of these two

Evidence from metaphors is slight, but it should be noted that
to the conventional metaphors utilizing the storm-tossed ship, the
fading flower, and the cruelty of the tiger, lion, and serpent which
the two plays have in common, *Conditions* adds at least a few
others which are less conventional: the judge presiding over a law
suit (ll. 644ff.), the rat who has tasted poison (ll. 732-36), and
additional metaphors in which figure the peacock, the merlin, and
the owl. Neither play, it should be noted, displays much ingenuity
in its manipulation of conventional figures.

Other details also argue against a theory of common authorship. In *Common Conditions*, for example, traditional misogyny
is expressed by two different characters – by Conditions, who
claims that women are "obscure and full of simpriety . . . slights
and fetches . . . fantasticall and full of variety strange"; and
Nomides, who lists the conventional representatives of inconstancy
and deceit – Helen, Cressida, Phaedra – and concludes that
women "all deceitfull bee". The author of *Clyomon and Clamydes*,
on the other hand, has omitted a similar passage which appears in
his source, *Perceforest*. There the Chevalier Dore (Clyomon in
the play) is warned about the deceitfulness of Nerones who, his
informant claims, did not resist the attempt of the King of Norway to abduct her and who is, hence, a representative of the
typical "subtilz . . . & malicieux que femmes treuvent a besoing
ains quelles ne parviennent a leur intention".[15]

In their construction, the two plays show at least two significant differences. One is that the action in *Common Conditions* is
repeatedly initiated by the Vice: he is responsible for the banish-
ment of Galiarbus and the flight of Sedmond and Clarisia; he
elicits the jealousy of the Duchess of Phrygia which prompts the
flight of Clarisia and Lamphedon; and he administers the poison

---

plays and of *Cambises* is based solely on the evidence of proverbial material (proverbs, sententious remarks, and comparisons). He concludes that
the possibility "that all three plays were written by Preston seems less likely
than that the two later productions were the work of a school of which he
was the founder. B. J. Whiting, *Proverbs in the Earlier English Drama*
(Cambridge, 1938), p. 294.
[15] *Perceforest*, Vol. III, Chapter 34.

to Clarisia (Metrea) and Lamphedon just before the play breaks off. Thus Conditions' role as chief intriguer is in contrast to Subtle Shift's; only once does Shift initiate action – in his betrayal of Clamydes to Bryan Sans Foy – for Shift is primarily a comic character.

The difference between the two Vices extends beyond their relations to plot to their actual characterization. Conditions is equipped with various tag-lines which do not appear in *Clyomon and Clamydes*, and there is some reason to think that his role was conceived for a specific actor. His tag-lines include the traditional "this gear cottons" or "this gear fauls out excellent well" – an idiom which occurs four times in the play. To this is added the characteristic "Welfare olde shift at a neede", "Welfare a craftie knaue at a time of neede", "Well fare at a pinche euermore", and "Welfare a head that can bryng sutch things in minde". And Conditions has other tag lines: he twice says he will "lay all care in the dust" (ll. 116 and 401) and he comments several times that events are "at a mad kinde of stay". Thus while Conditions shares with Shift the oaths and tricks that characterize the traditional Vice, his character is further distinguished by certain tag-lines which are not a part of the dramatic role of the other Vice.

The part of Conditions may also have been written for a particular actor, for the text repeatedly refers to his size. He is "goodman squat", and "elfe". He says of himself "was there euer little knaue driuen to hang himself", "of a littel man where I hit I breake the bone", and "tis a wonder that sutch strength in a littel mans arme should be".[16] The role of course may have been intended for a boy, but it is more probable that this, the lead role, was intended for one of the principal adult actors of a professional troupe, a comedian whose size was an essential part of his comic stock-in-trade.

In at least one other respect the plays are different in construction. *Common Conditions* contains eleven scenes in which three or more characters engage in dialogue. *Clyomon and Clamydes* has only five such scenes and in these the exchange is dialogue in name only, for minor characters usually speak only

16 See ll. 407, 1004, 1016, 1579, 1733.

one or two lines in response to the speeches of the major characters. It has already noted that *Conditions* tends to dispense with
the fourteener in passages which consist of rapid exchanges of
dialogue. And perhaps the inference should be that this writer's
sense of the dramatic prompted his preference for the colloquial in
tone and for the informal in situation.

Such, then, is the evidence that may be adduced concerning the
common authorship of these two plays of which the surface
similarities are obviously rather great. And while the question of
common authorship of *Common Conditions* and *Clyomon and
Clamydes* is negligible inasmuch as the author must in any event
remain anonymous, its resolution does have significance for literary history. For if these two romantic plays are by different
authors – and internal evidence suggests that they are – this knowledge makes us better able to discern, by a little, something of the
common stylistic, structural and thematic properties of the writers
of romantic drama during the seventies.

3

DATE

All students of the drama – with the single exception of Creizenach [1] – agree that *Clyomon and Clamydes* belongs somewhere in the decade of the seventies. Fleay, for example, suggests the date 1570 or 1578 – the years, he says, of the original production and revival of *Cambises*.[2] Both Chambers [3] and Harbage suggest 1570, though Harbage gives the limiting dates 1570-1583.[4] Greg implies a date c. 1576, saying that *Clyomon and Clamydes* is contemporary with and "if anything, probably anterior to *Common Conditions*" (S.R. 1576).[5] And the Shakespeare Institute's file of dated plays gives the date c. 1580.

In spite of the general agreement that the play should be placed in the 1570's, the whole matter is admittedly conjectural; and it is complicated by the fact that the only external evidence – the title-page – suggests an anterior limit of 1583, while internal evidence – for example the fourteener, rhetorical rather than dramatic structure, the appearance of a Vice, the presence of personifications – suggests an earlier date of composition. Thus the available evidence, which is limited, appears to be conflicting,

---

[1] Creizenach contends that the publication date – 1599 – represents the approximate date of the play's composition and that it is thus "a mere straggler left behind by a tendency already passed away". Wilhelm Creizenach, *The English Drama in the Age of Shakespeare* (London, 1916), p. 18.
[2] Fleay, *op. cit.*, II, 296.
[3] Chambers, *op. cit.*, IV, 6.
[4] Alfred Harbage, *Annals of the English Drama 975-1700*, revised by S. Schoenbaum (London, 1964), p. 40.
[5] W. W. Greg (ed.), *Sir Clyomon and Sir Clamydes* (Malone Society Reprint, 1913), p. vi.

and one is left with the vague supposition that the play belongs somewhere in the period c. 1570-1583.

External evidence is limited to the title-page statement that the play "hath bene sundry times Acted by her Majesties Players". The company referred to is presumably the Queen's company, which was organized by Walsingham in March of 1583; and, in the absence of other evidence, that year might serve as the limiting date for its earliest production were it not for the fact that title-page ascriptions commonly designate the last company to which a play belonged. But even if one allows for the possibility that the Queen's company founded in 1583 might have taken over the play from another company, a study of those features on the text which indicate the company and stage for which the play was originally written suggests not only that it was written for one of the regular companies but also that it was intended for production in one of the regular theaters and hence establishes an ultimate anterior limit of 1576 for the play's production if not for its composition.

Most important is evidence for the use of suspension gear or a lift about two-thirds of the way through the play when Providence enters with the direction *"Descend Providence"* and then, 14 lines later, exits with the direction *"Ascend"* (sc. xviii). Of course mechanical contrivances whereby gods – or clouds or animals for that matter – were let down from an upper level had been in use on the pageant stage since the fourteenth century; [6] and similar mechanisms whereby gods were let down from the theater "heavens" were to become a favorite spectacle with public theater audiences so that by 1598, Ben Jonson could complain, in the Prologue of *Every Man in His Humour*, of that portion of common theatrical fare when the "creaking throne comes down the boys to please". But in the early days of the professional stage, the employment of suspension gear was necessarily confined to the regular theaters, and hence the directions for the descent and ascent in *Clyomon and Clamydes* furnish substantial evidence for connecting that play with one of the regular theaters – The Theatre or the "first"

[6] Glynne Wickham, *Early English Stages 1300-1600* (London, 1959), I, 93-99.

or "early" Blackfriars (1576) or The Curtain (1577). The definite-
ness of the directions, moreover, suggests the bookkeeper's hand
and hence strengthens the supposition that the play (or this
portion of it) was prepared for production in a regular theater;
for they contrast strikingly with fairly common directions, presumably authorial, which call for descents and ascents if they are possible. The direction at the end of *Alphonsus, King of Aragon*, is an
example: *"Exit* Venus. *Or if you can conveniently, let a chair come
down from the top of the stage, and draw her up"* (ll. 2109-2110).

Unfortunately, no evidence has survived to indicate which of
the early theaters was equipped with suspension gear and hence
which one might have housed the earliest production of *Clyomon
and Clamydes*. Yet it is fairly certain, because of its style and
subject matter, that the play belonged to the popular theater.[7] And
the fact that public and private theater plays produced before
1608 are differentiated by the regular division of the private
theater plays into acts [8] – a practice which reflects the regular use
of inter-act as opposed to "dramatic" music in the private theaters [9] – lends added support to the theory that *Clyomon and
Clamydes*, an undivided play with no indication of inter-act
music, was written for production in one of the public theaters.
Thus the anterior limit for the play's production may be set with
some certainty at 1576, the year when James Burbage constructed
The Theatre, or at the latest, at 1577, when The Curtain was
constructed.[10] And perhaps the hypothesis most consistent with the

[7] If the playwright uses the terms "pageant" and "motions" in a technical, theatrical sense, they provide further evidence for the play's connection with a regular theater. See note to ll. 2131-35, p. 184.
[8] Wilfred T. Jewkes, *Act Division in Elizabethan and Jacobean Plays
1583-1616* (Hamden, Connecticut, 1958), pp. 96-102.
[9] Richard Hosley, "Was There a Music Room in Shakespeare's Globe?"
ShS, XIII (1960), 116-117.
[10] The only collateral evidence for the date of the play coincides with this
estimate. This is the paraphrase in the play (ll. 992-1001) of Lord Vaux's
lyric "No pleasure without some paine," which was first published in *The
Paradise of Dainty Devices* (1576). The lost play *The Red Knight*, which
was performed some time between July 29 and August 5, 1576 by the
Chamberlain's (Sussex') men in Bristol may *conceivably* be associated with
the brief episode of "le chevalier a lescu vermeil" which is told in Vol. III,
Chapters 129, 132-134 of *Perceforest*.

textual hypothesis – a composite of prompt book and foul papers – is one that postulates a public-theater play dating back as far as – but no further than – 1576, revived by the Queen's Men after 1583, sold by that same company to Thomas Creede some time around 1593/4, and printed in 1599 by Creede as he received it from the company.

4

STAGING AND PRODUCTION

Although no stage history exists for *Clyomon and Clamydes* beyond the title-page ascription to the Queen's Men, the text itself provides the basis for speculation about some aspects of its staging and production. The staging must have involved the kind of foreshortening which Sidney describes in *An Apology for Poetry* when he speaks of a stage with "Asia of one side, and Affrick of the other", for in spite of numerous changes of locale indicated by the dialogue, their variety is limited. The scene changes from Denmark to Swavia, thence to Macedon, Swavia, the Forest of Marvels (which is "in the way" from Swavia to Macedon), the Ile of Strange Marshes, a forest near the Norwegian court, the Ile of Strange Marshes again, and finally Denmark. Out of the confusion, however, emerge three generalized localities – a court, a forest, and unspecified roads which the characters travel.[1] Of these, only the forest may have required scenery, through references to it in the dialogue and in one stage direction – *"Enter* Neronis *in the Forrest"*. . . – may be no more than attempts to establish locality imaginatively, as frequently in the dialogue: "heere this forrest", "hard by in the Forrest heere", "let us go furder into the woods", "in this forrest", and so on.[2]

---

[1]   A forest, which was probably represented by a few stage trees, was also used in an "extended" sense to indicate scenes in a wilderness or on a sea shore. See G. F. Reynolds, " 'Trees' on the Stage of Shakespeare", *MP*, V (1907-8), 155-157.

[2]   Compare the references to the stage forest in *Timon of Athens*, IV, iii, 1: "Enter Timon in the woods", and in *2 Henry IV*, IV, i, with its reference to the forest of Gaultree. Such directions, which are probably more than place-indications, should be compared with the specification for practicable stage trees, as in *Common Conditions*, where Conditions "holoweth in the

On the other hand the play requires no "discovery" or use of a curtain; there is no action aloft and no action requiring the use of "houses" which figure so prominently in the Revels Accounts. The palace specified in scene viii does not need to be seen. And the castle mentioned in scenes vi, vii and x is apparently "within", for both stage directions and dialogue indicate that it is behind the door (or doors) at the back of the stage [3] – by inference, the tiring-house doors of a public theater.[4] A door also figures in Shift's first entrance: *"Here let him slip unto the Stage backwards, as though he had puld his leg out of the mire . . . and rise up to run in againe."* This appropriation of the theater doors for theatrical purposes is comparable to their use in *A Looking Glass for London and England*, for example, where Jonah is thrown on stage out of the whale's mouth (ll. 1450-51) or in *A Yorkshire Tragedy*, where the husband is thrown on stage off his horse: *"Enter Husband as being thrown off his horse, And falls"* (sc. viii).

Inferences that may be drawn about the production of the play are limited. Alterations and additions to the source underscore the probability of the play's actual connection with the Queen's Men, since they coincide with that company's preference for

---

tree" (l. 423), and for property trees as in *Old Fortunatus*, I, ii, where the stage directions call for *"a faire tree of Gold with apples on it"* and for a *"tree with greene and withered leaues mingled together, and little fruit on it. . . ."* The recent discovery of Adriaen van de Venne's illustration for *Tafereel* (1635) corroborates the evidence of stage directions and dialogue which indicate the use of property trees, for among other details, the illustration shows the tops of two stage trees back stage. (Richard Southern, "A 17th-Century Indoor Stage", *Theatre Notebook*, IX [1954], 8.) The whole subject of the stage forest is discussed by G. F. Reynolds, " 'Trees' on the Stage of Shakespeare", *op. cit.*, pp. 153-168.

[3] Stage directions include *Cary him out, Exit* (after Bryan has consented to let Shift guard Clamydes while he is in prison and says "Well then come follow after me . . ."), *Clamydes in prison*, and *Shift within*. Dialogue indicating that the prison is "within" includes Shift's lines "Ile open the prison doores", "looke out at the window", and "so the doores are open". Since Clamydes' part in this scene is too long to be spoken from behind the tiring house wall, the reference to the window may signify a grate or possibly an upper station from which he could speak his lines.

[4] Shift's line "Ile open the prison doores" is consistent with Johannes de Witt's sketch of The Swan, which shows that both of the tiring house doors were, in fact, double doors.

plays with two major comics and more than one leading role.[5] Hence the playwright's mingling of the Clamydes-Juliana episode with the more popular Clyomon-Nerones episode and his addition of the Vice (Shift) and the Rustic (Corin) seem to be more than merely gratuitous.[6] Otherwise the casting pattern yields few inferences. It required probably ten actors – seven men and three boys.[7] A possible division of parts which takes into account the limitations of doubling can be charted thus:

I. CLAMYDES: i, iii, v, vii, x xiv, xxii, xxiii
II. CLYOMON: ii, iii v, viii, xvi, xix, xxii, xxiii
III. SHIFT: ii, iii, v, vi, vii, x, xiv, xvi, xvii, xxii, xxiii
IV. 1. Lord: iii, iv, xxii, xxiii; Servant: vii; Boatswain: viii; Knight: x; Thrasellus: xiii-xvi
V. Prologue; 2. Lord: iii, xii, xxii; BRYAN: vi, vii, xxi, xxiii; Rumor: xiii; Providence: xviii
VI. 3. Lord: iii, viii, xii, xvi, xxiii; Servant: vii; Mustantius: xxii; CORIN: xv, xvi
VII. King of Suavia: iii; Alexander: iv, xxii; Lord: viii, xvi; Knight: x; King of Denmark: xxiii
1. NERONIS: viii, xi, xv, xviii, xx, xxii, xxiii
2. JULIANA: i, xxiiii; Herald: iii; Lady: vii
3. Lady: viii; Queen of the Strange Marshes: xxii; Queen of Denmark: xxiii

On the whole, props are simple, the only ones requiring special preparation being the serpent's head, the hearse (i.e. coffin), and perhaps the golden and silver shields which identify the two heroes. Otherwise props are items that would be readily available – a sheep hook, a "bag as it were full of gold", a mace, swords, shields, and the like. Sound effects are used sparingly and are specified only by one line of dialogue – "sound your Drums and Trumpets both" – and by three stage directions – *"Sing heere", "Sound heere once"* and, two lines later, *"Sound second time"*. (The reference to a storm at ll. 724 and 727 and

---

[5] T. W. Baldwin, *On the Literary Genetics of Shakespere's Plays* (Urbana, Illinois, 1959), pp. 200-213; 233 ff.
[6] See Introduction, pp. 44-45.
[7] The standard size of the professional troupe during the first half of Elizabeth's reign was ordinarily limited to from four to to six players. W. J. Lawrence, *Pre-Restoration Stage Studies* (Cambridge, Massachusetts, 1927), pp. 43-46.

to a "fight within" at l. 940 presumably also required some back-stage sound effects.)

Costumes, on the other hand, may have been more elaborate than the text suggests, for the play presents four full court scenes and characters appearing in a variety of costume – mariner, shepherd, page, whiffler – besides characters like Rumor and Providence who probably required some kind of traditional costume identified with the role.

5

SOURCES

a. *Perceforest*

The material for the double love-plot of *Clyomon and Clamydes* comes from three distinct episodes in the second and third volumes of *Perceforest*,[1] an anonymous French prose romance of the fourteenth century.[2] Something of the popularity of the romance in the sixteenth century may be inferred from its publication in France in 1528 and again in 1532, its translation into Italian by one Michele Tramezzino and its publication in Italy in 1558, and the publication of a detached episode – "La plaisante et amoureuse histoire du Chevalier Dore et de la pucelle surnomme Cuer d'acier" – in Paris in 1542.[3] Though the playwright makes full

---

[1] L. M. Ellison, *The Early Romantic Drama at the English Court* (Menasha, Wisconsin, 1917), pp. 113-127. The full title reads: La Treselegante, Delicieuse, Melliflue et Tresplaisant Hystoire du tresnoble Victorieux et excellentissimi roy Perceforest, Roy de la grant Bretaigne, fundateur du Franc palais et du temple du souuerain dieu. En laquelle le lecteur pourra veoir la source et decoration de toute Chevalerie, Culture de vraye Noblesse, Prouesse et conquestes infinies, accomplies des le temps du conquerant Alexandre le grant, et de Julius cesar au par avant la nativite de nostre soulueur Jesuchrist.
[2] *Perceforest* was conceived as a sequel to *Vœux du Paon*, written by Jacques de Longuyon c. 1313, and hence in attempts to date it, c. 1313 is the anterior limit. Gaston Paris suggests c. 1340 as the probable date of composition. ("Le Conte de la Rose dans le roman de *Perceforest*", *Romania*, XIII [1884], 480-84.) L. F. Flutre substantiates this conclusion in "Etudes sur le roman de *Perceforest*, Premier Article", *Romania*, LXX (1948-9), 480-81. A more recent estimate – between 1313 and 1323 – is suggested by Jeanne Lods in *Le Roman de Perceforest* (Geneva, 1951), pp. 276-77.
[3] The detached episode is dated earlier – between 1480 and 1490 – but

use of the Chevalier Dore-Cuer d'acier episode, his source was the
full length romance.

The principal changes wrought on the source material appear to
stem from an impulse toward order and symmetry, a need for
dramatization and a response to audience demands for romantic
heroine and comic figure. For three characters in the romance —
Lionnel du Glar, Clamides and Bethides — the play has only Clamydes; and for two others — Bruyant Sans Foy and Harban the
imposter — it has simply Bryan Sans Foy. From the numerous
episodes that make up its plot in the romance, the playwright has
selected only the high points for dramatization. And for the
courtly Nerones and genteel hermit of *Perceforest* he has substi-
tuted the "new woman" — independent, aggressive, almost auda-
cious — and the rustic Corin, whom he balances with still another
comic addition, Subtle Shift the Vice.

Probably the most significant alterations that the playwright
makes in his source, however, are the more intangible shifts in
tone and emphasis that transform an atmosphere congenial to
romance — urbane, courtly, alternately witty and sober, but always decorously so — into a self-conscious courtliness and high-
mindedness relieved only by the broad and obvious humor of the
Vice and the Rustic. Where the romance writer takes as his
province "la source et decoration de toute chevalerie, Culture de
vraye Noblesse, Prouess et conquestes infinies" from the time of
Alexander the Great to King Arthur, the playwright's more
modest claim is to show "the Glasse of glory" wherein one may see
the vagaries of both Fortune and Love and the "just reward" of
both honorable and "ignomius" actions. Hence the characters
generally undergo deflation in their transposition from the romance
to the play: the daughter of the Fairy Queen becomes the daughter
to the King of Denmark, an ancient hermit of obvious blood and
breeding becomes Corin, the rustic, and the arch-enemy of all of
the knights of the Franc Palais, a powerful enchanter who is the

---

it evidently was plagiarized from the original edition of 1528 or from the
reprint of 1531, a fact that the editor tried to conceal by changing the
name of Perceforest to Peleon. (Flutre, *op. cit.*, p. 478.) For a list of the
extant manuscripts as well as the editions in print, see Flutre's article,
pp. 475-61.

only descendent of the enchanter Darnant, becomes the cowardly, "ignomius" Bryan Sans Foy, whose enchantments make up for his "want of valiancie". In fact, the marvellous that pervades *Perceforest* – enchantments, prophetic dreams, marvellous beasts and the like – is reduced in the play to one enchantment. And this reduction is part and parcel with the love-longings and laments and the stylized humor (e.g. the Chevalier Dore's retreat to a large wardrobe when Nerones' father appears suddenly at her door) that disappear in the stage version. A summary of the relevant episodes from *Perceforest* with an indication of the playwright's use of them will indicate something of the direction and intent of his alterations and additions.

The first plot combines two separate episodes from *Perceforest* – one concerning Lyonnel du Glar's pursuit of Blanche, daughter of the Fairy Queen and Gadiffer, and the other concerning the enmity between Bethides, the "Blanc Chevalier", and Blanche's brother Nestor, the "Chevalier Dore".

Lyonnel's story is about his quest for the Giant with the Golden Hair. Only if he is able to bring the Giant's head as a trophy to the Fairy Queen will he be able to win Blanche's hand. Armed with a shield depicting both the object and reward of his quest and accompanied by his faithful squire Clamides, Lyonnel sets forth, but his quest proves to be long and difficult, for twice he is distracted by adventures that appeal to his sense of knightly obligation. First is his encounter with a lion and lioness who for fifty years have been ravaging the Kingdom of the Strange Marches and whom he determines to kill. He accomplishes the feat but is badly wounded and, as a result, is taken to the principal castle of the realm, where he remains until he recovers.

Setting out again in search of the Giant, Lyonnel and Clamides next meet an old man, the mariner Nabin, who promises to take them to their destination. Before they can complete their voyage, however, they must sail past an island inhabited by a flying serpent – a beast which has spread such terror among the mariners that none of them dares sail the seas surrounding his abode. Thus once again Lyonnel undertakes to rid society of a brute terror and once again, of course, he is successful.

With the sea now open, Lyonnel arrives in the land dominated
by the Giant, seeks him out, and slays him. After his squire Clamides marries the Giant's daughter, Lyonnel re-embarks, accompanied now by a lion cub that he had taken from the Kingdom of
the Strange Marches and carrying trophies of his various adventures – the feet of the lion and the serpent and the head of the
Giant with the Golden Hair. His return, however, proves to be
as difficult as his quest, for he soon enters the Forest of Marvels,
where he is deprived first of the shield Blanche had given him and
then of the trophies which were to give proof of his successful ac-
complishment of the quest. In his sorrow, Lyonnel composes a "lay
de complaincte", which he charges a minstrel to sing in his travels
through the realm. Fortunately the minstrel makes his way to the
court of the Fairy Queen, where Blanche hears him and charges
him to return with a "lay de confort" which informs her knight of
recent events in fairy land: the deception practised by Harban, "le
faulx chevalier", who has presented Lyonnel's trophies to the
Queen as though they were his own, the Fairy Queen's divination
of his imposture, and the subsequent erection of the "temple de la
franche garde" in honor of the unknown knight whose trophies
Harban has stolen.

From another informant, Lyonnel learns that the temple, which
is guarded by his lion, houses the trophies of his quest and that it
is so constructed that only their legitimate owner will be able to
enter and recover them. In possession of this knowledge, Lyonnel
makes his way to the temple, recovers his trophies, and presents
them to the Fairy Queen, who receives him with great honor. Yet
even now he is not to receive his reward, for the Queen imposes a
waiting period on him in punishment for his initial loss of the
shield and the trophies.

During the interim, Lyonnel undertakes to enter a tournament
at the request of Gadiffer, but his travels are again frought with
difficulty, for he encounters a woman by means of whose machina-
tions he is imprisoned in the castle of Bruyant Sans Foy, the only
living descendant of the enchanter Darnant. In prison, Lyonnel
meets other famous knights of the realm – Estonne, le Tors de
Pedrac, Troylus, and Zelandine – who have all similarly fallen

into the snares of "mauvaisez femmes". But Lyonnel is Bruyant's chief prisoner, for as the descendant of Belinant du Glar who brought about the destruction of Darnant and his progeny he bears the brunt of Bruyant's hatred. Before Bruyant can carry out his revenge, however, the knights of the Franc Palais are informed of their companions' distress and they come to the rescue, destroying Bruyant's men and putting Bruyant himself to flight.

Though Lyonnel's subsequent adventures make up a large part of volume III of the romance, the play passes over these, using only his final reunion with Blanche and their marriage, which occurs at the beginning of volume IV.

The character Clamydes in the play is based primarily, then, on Lyonnel du Glar; but in order to connect this plot with the Clyomon-Neronis plot, the playwright transferred the actions of a second character, Bethides, to Lyonnel.[4] This episode describes how Bethides – the "Blanc Chevalier" – was to receive the order of knighthood, how the ceremony was interrupted by a strange knight, the "Chevalier Dore", and how the two knights subsequently resolved their enmity.[5] The playwright follows this episode closely, arranging however that the knight meet for a trial by combat in Macedon (rather than at the Pine of Marvels) and changing the dispute over the crown from the land of Borras to the Ile of Strange Marches.

The second plot of the play – the Clyomon-Neronis plot – is based on the episode concerning Nestor, the brother of Blanche, who is known as the "Chevalier Dore".[6] Arriving at the Pine of

[4] Bethides, who is a son of Perceforest, falls in love with Cerse la Romaine, who has left her homeland to follow a squire named Luce. At first Perceforest refuses Bethides permission to marry her, but he finally relents and a feast is organized for their nuptials. But dire omens accompany the nuptials and not long afterwards Cerse meets Luce and promises to deliver the British up to the Roman legions. By a substitution of letters, she attracts from their posts the knights of the Franc Palais and the defenders of Scotland, bringing about their defeat at the hands of the Romans. (Vol. IV.)

[5] The Lyonnel-Blanche story appears in Volume II, chapters 33, 46-49, 57-61, 75-84, 91-104; and in Volume III, chapters 12-14, 19-20, 22-23, 25, 53. The Blanc Chevalier-Chevalier Dore episode appears in Volume II, chapters 142-43 and in Volume III, chapters 7 and 40.

[6] The Chevalier Dore-Neronis story appears in Volume III, chapters 5, 33-38, 40, 42.

Marvels to joust with the Blanc Chevalier, the Chevalier Dore is mysteriously wounded and miraculously transported by the spirit Zephyr to a garden near the principal castle in the Kingdom of the Strange Marches. Though the King of the Strange Marches keeps his daughter Nerones a virtual prisoner in the castle, she sees the wounded knight and contrives to have him brought there in secret so that she can nurse him back to health. During his long convalescence, the Chevalier Dore and Nerones fall in love, but numerous obstacles make their immediate marriage impossible: Nerones is being wooed by the King of Norway and her father favors the alliance; and the Chevalier Dore, who is still obliged to joust with the Blanc Chevalier, refuses to reveal his name until he has vanquished his foe – a refusal which Nerones considers a "grant follie" but which the knight insists on. Thus the two gentles confess their mutual love and the Chevalier Dore, promising to return in sixty day's time, leaves to seek out the Blanc Chevalier.

During his absence Nerones is wooed by Fergus, King of Norway, who undertakes the defense of an island in order to win her, loses patience, and kidnaps her. Nerones escapes from him by feigning death and fleeing from her coffin under cover of night. Making her way to a farmhouse, she takes refuge with an old woman who suggests that she disguise as a shepherd boy. The plan pleases Nerones, and she carries it out, assuming the name of Cœur Dacier as a sign of her faithfulness to her lover.

Meanwhile the Chevalier Dore journeys back to Great Britain in search of the Blanc Chevalier, and on his way he encounters various marvels, chief among them the "beste glatissant" which lives in the Forest du Glar. But before he arrives at his destination, a messenger from Nerones overtakes him, and he sets out for the Kingdom of the Strange Marches in order to meet his rival. Although he travels steadily night and day, he arrives too late to save Nerones from Fergus' treachery, and he sets out again in pursuit, overtaking Fergus finally as he sits beside Nerones' empty tomb and laments the duplicity of womankind. The Chevalier Dore easily downs Fergus' companions, but the King is his match and they do battle for all of one day before the Chevalier Dore finally defeats him and puts him to death. The knight is badly wounded, but happily an old man, a hermit, arrives on the scene and after helping the Chevalier Dore bury his enemy, he takes the knight to his lodging and there nurses him back to health. When he has recovered, the Chevalier Dore takes leave of the hermit, but at the man's request he leaves behind his armour and his weapons and assumes instead the guise of a shepherd. In this garb he takes lodging at the same farmhouse where Nerones, also disguised as a shepherd, has found refuge, but neither recognizes the other. Eventually he takes service with a knight named Pernahan and goes forth to fight and overthrow the giant Branq. After this feat, Cœur Dacier joins him as his squire and together they set out in search of the Blanc Chevalier. They arrive eventually in the land of Borras, where a dispute over the crown engages the Chevalier Dore's interest, and he offers his service in combat to one of the claimants. When the champion for the other claimant appears, it is the Blanc Chevalier. They engage in combat, but a slash in the Chevalier Dore's clothing reveals a birthmark which establishes his identity, and the two knights, who are cousins, are reconciled. The Chevalier Dore returns with Cœur Dacier to Scotland, where his mother penetrates the squire's disguise and the action closes with promise of the marriages that are performed in volume IV.

The most obvious differences between the characters and episodes of the romance and play appear to stem from the playwright's attempt to lessen the distance between his medieval material and classical technique. His alterations of names suggest this purpose (e.g. Lyonnel-Bethides to Clyomon, Fergus to Thrasellus, Blanche to Juliana and the Pine of Marvels to Macedon). But more important are his telescoping and compressing of characters in order to bring the two character groupings into sharp balance:

Alexander the Great

Clamydes (Lyonnel, Bethides)	hero	*Clyomon* (Nestor)
Juliana (Blanche)	heroine	*Neronis*
Bryan (Bruyant, Harban)	villain	*Thrasellus* (Fergus)
Shift (not in *Perceforest*)	comic character	*Corin (hermit, old woman)*

Queen of Denmark (Fairy Queen)	mother	Queen of Strange Marshes (not in Perceforest)
King of Denmark (Gadiffer)	father	Mustantius, uncle (Neron)

Still another evidence of the playwright's attempt to render his material correct classically is his strict adherence to the rules of decorum in the characterization of the lowly born (Shift and Corin). In *Perceforest*, when the characters happen to be lowly born (for example, the mariner Nabin) or when they follow lowly occupations (for example, the hermit who helps the Chevalier Dore bury his enemy Fergus) they are nevertheless true gentles. Corin, on the other hand, is a new creation, a rustic type whose abusive language, rambling idle gossip and lechery contrast strikingly with the asceticism of the hermit and with the idealized wise shepherd of the pastoral tradition in general. Corin himself notes the disparity between literary idealism and the actual life of the shepherd when he says mockingly

... tis a world to zee what mery lives we shepheards lead,
Why where Gentlemen and we get once a thorne bush over our head,
We may sleep with our vaces against the zone, and were hogs
Bath our selves, stretch out our legs ant were a cennell of dogs:
And then at night when maides come to milkin, the games begin.
                                                        (ll. 1293-97)

For his characterization, the author uses the central features of the southwestern dialect which had been the conventional literary dialect for rustics since around 1553,[7] and he carries out his depiction of the "natural" man in Corin's interest in neighbor Nichol's daughter, in neighbor Hodge's maid who "had a clap", his own doings with Frumpton's wench, his provincial admiration for "our Sir John the parish preest", and his assumption that all the world knows his little corner of England:

... our head controms wife, brother to my nabour *Nycholl*,
You know ha dwels by maister Justice, over the water on the other side of the hill,
Cham zure you know it, between my nabour *Filcher's* varme house,
    and the wind-mill.   (ll. 1399-1401)

[7] Eduard Eckhardt, *Die Dialekt- und Ausländerntypen des älteren Englischen Dramas* (Louvain, 1910), I, 4-79.

Still another alteration in the source, made presumably in the direction of probability, is the omission or alteration of virtually all episodes in Perceforest which depend on magic. Gone is Lyonnel's experience in the Forest of Marvels, for example, where he comes upon a great hall full of people which vanishes suddenly after he enters it.[8] Gone is the marvellous quest of the French Garde which was established by the Fairy Queen as a means of discovering the knight who had succeeded in killing the Giant with the Golden Hair.[9] Gone also are the clairvoyance of the Fairy Queen, the enchantment effected by the "mauvaise damoyselle", and, from the Chevalier Dore-Nerones plot, the motif of the two rings which the lovers exchange and which appear and disappear under remarkable circumstances.[10] And gone are episodes like the Chevalier Dore's encounter with the "beste glatissant".[11]

Other alterations of the source and additions to it reflect still other literary and social influences which intervened between the composition of *Perceforest* and *Clyomon and Clamydes*. The alteration in the play of the treatment of romantic love, for example, reflects the new Italianate mode in romantic literature from the middle of the century onward. Compare, for example, the scene where Lyonnel du Glar first sees Blanche with Clamydes' first meeting with Juliana. The story of Lyonnel's first sight of Blanche while she is bathing in a pool in the forest is a mixture of magic and fairy tale lore:

[He sees first the Fairy Queen] une dame de moult noble atour et de tresgrande beaulte ... et veit que la dame regardoit trois pucelles baignans en lestang si veit que cestoient trois les plus belles creatures quil eust oncques veues dont entre les autres en y avoit une si tres-

8   Volume II, chapter 75.
9   Volume II, chapter 93.
10   After the Chevalier Dore assumes the guise of a shepherd, he takes lodging with some country people. As it happens, Nerones has taken refuge in the same house. Because the Chevalier Dore does not know the ways of farming, he is given the task of caring for a lark that the rustics have captured. Not wanting the bird to escape, he ties the string that is fastened to its leg to the ring that Nerones had given him; but the lark flies away, taking the ring with it. After he goes in pursuit of the lark, Nerones is informed by a dream that the "varlet" was the Chevalier Dore and, joyous to learn that he is still alive, she sets out in search of him.
11   Volume III, chapter 34.

blanche quil sapensa qui cestoit chose face ne que chair humainne ne
povoit estre telle en blancheur ne en beaulte de visage . . . [He is interrupted by three knights who demand satisfaction for his gross im-
propriety of watching the maidens, and after he has done battle with
them he finds that the maidens have disappeared. He journeys on,
coming at last to a river.] Quant Lyonnel vint sur la riviere il sarresta
et puis regarde & veit au travers quatre damoiselles vestues dabitz plus
blancz que neige. Et si chevauchoient devant deux damoiseaulx
chascun son oyseau sur son poing montez richement. Quant Lyonnel
les veit il congneut tantost que cestoient les trois damoiselles quil
avoit veues baigner en lestang. [The river is too broad for him to
cross, however, and once again he loses sight of the maidens. He
rides on again until he is accosted by an old man who greets him
with these words:] "Chetif ou vas chetif que quiers." [Surprised,
Lyonnel asks him what he means.] "Je scay," dist il, "tant que se tu
suyz longuement ces damoyselles qui cy passent tu entereras en telle
amour dont tu te tiendras pour chetif." "Pourquoy beau sire," dist
Lyonnel, "me tiendray ie pour chetif." Adonc dist le bon preudhomme,
"pour les peines travaulx & meschancetez quil ten conviendra souf-
frir."[12]

Clamydes' meeting with Juliana has none of this fairy tale
quality. The opening passage (ll. 1-31) tells how he has arrived
in Denmark and there has fallen in love with the princess. It is
intended, apparently, to be both a realistic account of Clamydes'
difficult voyage and a metaphorical account of the progress of his
love for Juliana, for it is obviously a rendering of the popular
Petrarchan image of the mariner who was passed through the
storms of love to arrive finally at the harbour of the lady's mercy.[13]

The substitution of a newer literary mode for an older one is
particularly apparent in the playwright's transmutation of the
romantic heroine Nerones, who is conceived in terms of the conventions of courtly love in *Perceforest* but who reflects, in the play,
the tradition of the disguised innamorata of Italian *commedia erudita* and the amazonian heroine of renaissance epic.

The Nerones of *Perceforest*, in the tradition of the romance, is
kept a virtual prisoner in a castle surrounded by two rivers, and

---

[12]   Volume II, chapter 33
[13]   The ultimate source is Ariosto's "O sicuro, secreto e fidel porto" –
sonnet 3, Lirica. It was adapted by Drayton, no. 1, Constable, Dec. IV,
no. 3, Spenser lxiii, Smith xxxv, and Linche, xviii.

she can be taken from it only by the knight who will guard "lisle de
lespreuve" for sixty days, defending it from all other knights who
come to lay claim to her hand. Nerones' meeting with the Chevalier Dore is replete with the terms of courtly love. After his first
conversation with her, the Chevalier Dore begins to languish for
love of her invoking the aid "du dieu damors", feeling a "froidure . . .
par tout le corps", finds himself unable to sleep and finally in
danger of death if "la pucelle navoit mercy de luy". Though Nerones returns his love, she pretends indifference and even scorn
and "en ouvra tantost comme femme" until he dissolves in tears.
After the declaration of their mutual love, the affair continues in
the secrecy required by the scheme of courtly love, and Nerones'
one request of the Chevalier Dore when her father appears un-
expectedly is "saulvez mon honneur".

The Neronis of the play is altogether a different woman. In contrast to Nerones of the romance, whose father "voyant la grant
beaulte de sa fille la faisoit illec garder moult extroictement", she
makes her first appearance walking on the shore of her father's
kingdom in the company of lords and ladies of her court. When
she realizes her love for Clyomon, she declares herself in a scene
(xi) which contrasts strikingly in its candor with the love scene in
Perceforest. Her contemplation of suicide and her timely salvation
by Providence also contrast with the fortuitous discovery of Fergus'
tomb and of the Chevalier Dore's armour, which informs the
Nerones of the romance that her lover still lives. The play also
adds a suggestion of a motif popular in romantic comedy – the
wooing of the disguised heroine by another woman. The motif
remains undramatized in *Clyomon and Clamydes*, but Corin's remarks about his "boy Jacke" who is "plagely well lov'd in our
towne" suggest the seeds of that "romantic irony" which was to
become a staple of later comedy:

. . . and you did zee how *Jone Jenkin* and *Gilian Giffrey* love my boy
   Jacke,
Why it is marvelation to see, Jone did so bast *Gillians* backe,
That by Gos bones I laught till cha be pist my zelfe, when cha zaw it,
All the maides in towne valls out for my boy. . . .   (ll. 1405-8)

Perhaps the most striking measure of the difference between the two heroines is to be found in the final recognition scenes. In *Perce-forest* the Fairy Queen undertakes the task of revealing the true identity of the squire Cœur Dacier to her son Nestor, the Chevalier Dore. She takes him into a chamber where Nerones is bathing with the Queen's daughters and in a scene delightful for its humor and naivete convinces her son that his squire and the beautiful maiden before him are one and the same. In the play, on the other hand, the recognition scene (xxiii) is entirely of Neronis' own doing: she reveals her identity to the Queen of Denmark and then to Clyomon with the kind of initiative and candor common to the disguised heroine of renaissance comedy but completely lacking in the heroine of the romance.

b. *The Morality Play*

The playwright's other major alteration in his source is his addition of three figures from the morality play tradition – the personifications Rumor and Providence, and the Vice Subtle Shift. And while the juncture of morality and romance, of religious and secular themes and of the abstract and concrete in character produces what has been termed its "hybrid" quality,[14] the most distinctive result of this juncture and attempted fusion is the coloration that each mode takes from the other, the unavoidable shift in tone that occurs when one color, note, word or, in this case, artistic mode intersects another. To illustrate briefly, when the Vice, Subtle Shift, acts out his traditional role of the double-dealer, forsaking his masters, assuming a variety of disguises, acting always from the crassest and vilest of motives, he no longer personifies human concupiscence on the abstract stage of the psychomachia but he becomes instead an objective character, distinct in himself, whose motives must be rationalized and whose actions must be generated from within rather than from without. To put it differently, when the Vice enters the alien world of the romance, his transformation away from artificial abstraction and toward

[14] Bernard Spivack, *Shakespeare and the Allegory of Evil* (New York, 1958), p. 253.

naturalistic individual begins. And conversely, when the process of the humanization of characters – not only Shift, but Neronis and Corin as well – within the conventions of the romance begins, the values of that world as they are embodied in its artistic mode are opposed by characters whose very presence calls them into question. It is a process that foreshadows the collision of clowns, malcontents, and disguised heroines with princes and princesses in the Ardens and Illyrias to come – a process that contains the seeds of the kind of incongruity – the artificial, pretentious, and grandiose within the natural, simple, and normal doings of ordinary mortals – that we have come to label "comic".

The character Providence illustrates on a small scale the transformation of conventional figures when they appear in settings alien to them; for when Providence appears in sc. xviii not to save a sinner but to save a love-sick maiden, he has no more moral or theological significance than any other device – fortuitous discovery of a letter, entrance of another character – that might have been used to prevent the lady's untimely death. Deprived of the essential features of the morality play, Providence is nothing more than a stock figure, a literal *deus ex machina* whose descent and ascent, incidentally, added spectacle to one of the climactic scenes of the play.

In the character of the Vice, of course, the process of transformation implicit in his transference from homiletic to secular drama is much clearer; for while he retains the traditional trappings of the Vice's role, the motivations for that role inherent in the morality play are absent. Thus like the traditional Vice, Shift is a double-dealer whose deceit is emphasized by his pseudonym, Knowledge, intended to recommend him as a suitable guide, counselor, and servant for erring mankind, and by his various costume changes – from his first appearance as a traveller to his appearances as knight, fine gentleman, and finally whiffler. His double-dealing pervades the play, for he forsakes one master after another – first Clyomon, then Clamydes, and finally Bryan Sans Foy. To his masters he protests his honesty, declaring that "A true servant . . . will deceive his maister never", swearing to Clamydes "heeres my hand, ile deceive you never", and to Bryan, "Heres my hand,

charme, inchant, make a spider catcher of me if I be false to you
ever". To the audience, however, he proclaims his nature as a
"subtle shifting knave" who has a thousand shifts "to put myselfe
out of suspition" and to reap his own gain. The motivation behind
his deceit is primarily self-gain represented by two words – "com-
modity" and "advantage" – which appear frequently throughout
the play. Thus Shift declares that he will "for commoditie serve
every man", that "for advantage, [he] will deceive his owne
brother", or that, "like a shifting knave for advantage", he will
perform this or that action.

Deriving from the Vice's traditional role as interpreter of the
action are Shift's asides and addresses to the audience. He is the
only character in the play who addresses the audience directly in
order to explain the course of the action – what has happened behind the scenes or what is about to happen – or to announce his
plans. And following the constant rhetorical formula for the Vice,
he gives an exposition of his name and nature:

> Subtill Shift I am called, that is most plaine,
> And as it is my name, so it is my nature also
> To play the shifting knave wheresoever I go.   (ll. 212-14)

While Shift retains some of the characteristic features of the Vice,
he nevertheless exemplifies the kind of changes that the secular
drama imposed on the traditional role. Most important is the fact
that his name has ceased to have metaphorical significance. If he
is a knave and a villain, he is so objectively and literally rather than
metaphorically. Thus he is imbued with motivations which over-
lay his traditional amorality. He aligns himself with Bryan out of
fear and out of a sense of kinship with a fellow coward. And he
rescues Clamydes from Bryan's castle because of contempt for
Bryan and because of remorse. When Shift muses, "what a villain
am I my maister to betray" or "Am I not worthie to be hangd", he
exemplifies the humanizing and literalizing of the traditionally
amoral Vice that his appearance in the secular drama demanded.

The other significant change wrought in the Vice by his appearance in the secular drama is his enmity toward values – social,
political, educational, romantic – other than the ethical and moral

values of the morality play. Like Bryan and Thrasellus, Shift is numbered among the "ignomius" persons mentioned in the prologue who serve as foils for the chivalric ideals of courage, loyalty, and love. To his lack of loyalty implicit in his role as double-dealer and his self-professed cowardice are added his lust and lasciviousness. His comments on love have consistently the double-edged ring of the sexual entendre. He is first discovered "in a dirtie Ditch with a woman", and he introduces himself as Knowledge, which means, he says, "good skill in a woman".

Shift, then, is the Vice in a dramatic sense only. Transferred to the world of the chivalric romance, he becomes a comic, low-life figure who acts as a foil to the values it advances. Retaining the traditional trappings of his role, he is nevertheless little more than a harmless intriguer and necessary narrator whose actions have little effect on the movement of the play.

Taken together, the alterations in the romance material and additions to it indicate not so much artlessness, which is the charge usually levelled at the early romantic drama, as its reverse. In the playwright's attempts to bring order and symmetry to the plot and decorum to his characters, probability to his actions and probity to his characters, he produced the kind of stilted formality that one usually associates with a Huanebango or a Pistol in later drama. Yet the alterations are significant for the development of romantic comedy. For the double-plot structure and characters like Shift, Corin and Neronis illustrate the conventions on which comedy was to be built. Though their conventional features are dominant in *Clyomon and Clamydes*, they foreshadow the clowns, malcontents and disguised heroines of later comedy whose presence was to dissolve the romance structure, calling into question its values, rendering its assumptions and conventions comic when seen in the perspective of actual human behavior.

6

CLYOMON AND CLAMYDES: AN EARLY ROMANTIC PLAY

a. The Early Romantic Drama

Clyomon and Clamydes, Common Conditions, and *The Rare Triumphs of Love and Fortune* are the only surviving representatives of a large group of romantic plays which were produced during the period from about 1570 to about 1585. The facts relating to this body of romantic drama are given in Appendix B. They indicate that almost one-third of the plays which were produced and/or printed during this period were based on romance material – a useful reminder, as Harbage points out, "that dragons, enchanters, armored knights, and damsels in distress peopled the English stage for a considerable period of time".[1] Yet three extant plays and the titles of 27 lost plays furnish little evidence on which to base a definition and evaluation; and contemporary criticism, which evaluates the romantic drama in terms of neo-classical criteria, does little to clear away our confusion and downright ignorance about the genre. For, granted its fantastic plot, exotic setting, and confused time sequence, granted its stereotyped characters, traditional motifs, and multiple plot, enumeration of these qualities fails to suggest its nature as a dramatic type.

It is, in fact, in regard to the nature of the romantic play that contemporary criticism – particularly the often quoted passages from Whetstone, Gosson, and Sidney – is liable to be misleading, for although contemporary critics describe with some accuracy the material of the romantic drama, they suggest an artlessness which

[1] Alfred Harbage, *Shakespeare and the Rival Traditions* (New York, 1952), p. 62.

is not entirely borne out by an examination of the evidence. Moreover, it is not the material to which these critics object but the handling of the material, the failure of the playwrights to order their material according to neoclassical dicta which required adherence to the unities and the laws of decorum and, above all, conformity to the dictum that art must both teach and delight. Thus George Whetstone, in his *Epistle* to William Fleetwood appended to *Promos and Cassandra* (1578), complains that the English playwright

... fyrst groundes his worke on impossibilities; then in three howres ronnes he throwe the worlde, marryes, gets Children, makes Children men, men to conquer kingdomes, murder Monsters, and bringeth Gods from Heauen, and fetcheth Diuels from Hel.[2]

But he adds, significantly, that "their ground is not so vnperfect, as their workinge indiscreete: ..." And this bad "workinge" he identifies as their failure to observe the rules of decorum and to order their works so that "the graue matter may instruct, and the pleasant delight; ..."

Similarly Gosson, in *Plays Confuted in Five Actions* (1583), complains about the "aduentures of an amorous knight, passing from countrie to countrie for the loue of his lady, encountring many a terible monster made out of broune paper ..." – but his chief concern is that such plays teach nothing.[3] And Sidney, describing the absurdities of the romantic play in the *Apology for Poetry* (1583) is concerned not with the material but with the writers' failure to observe the unities of time and place, their breach of decorum in the mingling of the tragic and comic, and their failure to produce the "delightful teaching which is the end of Poesie".[4]

---

[2] Epistle to William Fleetwood, *The Historie of Promos and Cassandra*, in *Elizabethan Critical Essays*, ed. G. Gregory Smith (Oxford, 1904), I, 59.
[3] Chambers, *Elizabethan Stage*, IV, 215.
[4] Jonson's criticism of the romantic drama in *The Magnetic Lady*, I, Chorus, 15-24, might be added. To Mr. Damplay's criticism that the first act should have more action, a second speaker replies: "... if a Child could be borne, in a *Play*, and grow up to a man, in the first Scene before hee went off the Stage: and then after to come forth a Squire, and bee made a Knight: and that Knight to travell betweene the Acts, and doe

While such criticism indicates the failure of the playwrights to follow acceptable dramaturgical conventions, it should not be taken to indicate complete artlessness. Rather, it is possible to see in the extant plays representing the early romantic drama an attempt to solve the problems of structure and language in terms consistent with their material rather than in terms supplied by humanistic criticism. Such material implied a certain artistic method, one that had been perfected in prose narrative but that required adjustment if it was to be transferred to poetic drama. It demanded solution of the problems of time, place and characterization other than that of the morality play on the one hand and of the classical drama on the other. Diverse characters, multiple plots, exotic action and settings required a unity of theme and impression rather than a unity of action. Or stated differently, the romantic material demanded the creation of suitable techniques, the creation of a different artistic reality; and if *Clyomon and Clamydes* fails as a work of art, it is not because its author gave himself over to undisciplined flights of fancy but because he had not yet solved the problems inherent in the dramatization of the loosely constructed, episodic romance – problems that were to be solved by a later generation of dramatists who would use the material first as the basis for romantic comedy and later for dramatic romance.

b. *Style*

Much of the apparent artificiality and ineptness of *Clyomon and Clamydes* stems from the tradition of the romance. Like *Perceforest*, the play represents the kind of artistic expression that is general rather than particular – one that idealizes a particular social milieu, that seeks to sustain a set of generally accepted

---

wonders i' the holy land, or else where; kill Paynims, wild Boores, dun Cowes, and other Monsters; beget him a reputation, and marry an Emperours Daughter for his Mistres; convert her Fathers Countrey; and at last come home, lame, and all to be laden with miracles" – then such a play might please Damplay and "the People" (in *Works*, eds. C. H. Herford, Percy and Evelyn Simpson [Oxford, 1938], VI, 527-528).

values and expresses these values through a group of representative characters whose sentiments are also representative and general rather than particular. Like the writer of the romance, the playwright has little interest in time sequence and realistic setting, in individual emotions and character motivation – in any of those elements which would contribute to "naturalistic" drama. Rather, he is interested in plot and character only as they reflect an ideal of life which is noble, refined, and moral. That is, like the romance writer before him, he accepts generalities of character and values as true and valid, not because they have any real contact with human nature, but because they have contact with the social world – the source of order and continuity, of traditions, manners and morals – which to him are infinitely more significant than mere individual eccentricity. And the result of his interest in the general and representative is a drama which is formal and stylized, which is not to our way of thinking "dramatic" at all because it lacks the dynamic inherent in the conflict between characters and, on another level, between contrasting concepts of reality.

Throughout, the play illustrates this devotion to the general and representative inherent in its source. Certain ideals – for example, courage, honor, loyalty, service to women – are reiterated, first by one character, then another, and it matters little to whom the sentiments are assigned. The chivalric code demands that Clamydes act "in hope of honours Crowne", or to "winne Dame Honours Crowne", that Clyomon seek "to winne the brute of Fame", that the King of Swavia explain the object of knighthood to be "that honour thine may flow . . . to thy immortal fame". Since the code of love demands unswerving loyalty, Clamydes protests to Juliana, "I am thine til fates untwine of vital life the stay", and Clyomon promises Neronis "whilest that life doth last thine faithfull to remaine". Both Clyomon and Alexander are assigned speeches celebrating the glory of battle and conquest. The King of Denmark describes the obligations of knighthood, and Alexander enunciates the duty of the King as ideal judge. It matters little whether these speeches are assigned to king or knight; the sentiments are suitable to all of the major characters.

And the "ignomius" characters mentioned in the prologue – Shift, Corin, the King of Norway – are simply those whose erring attitudes toward the accepted values mark them as foils to the major characters.

Also inherent in the romance material is a singular lack of interest in characterization. The major figures in the play are, of course, stock figures – king, knight, lady, enchanter, villain. Like the figures of the romance, they are defined only in their relation to a plot whose conventional situations and motifs – e.g. quest, enchantment, challenge to combat demand certain obvious responses. The emotions expressed by the characters are always stereotyped and generalized – joy and grief, love and hate, courage and fear. Motives are limited to the most basic ones – love again, hate, desire for revenge, concern for honor. Comparison of the laments spoken by the heroes when each discovers that he will not be able to meet his adversary before Alexander on the appointed day illustrates their completely generalized, representative quality. Both knights inveigh against the vagaries of Fortune. Thus Clyomon:

What greater griefe can grow to gripe, the heart of greeved wight,
Then thus to see fell *Fortune* she, to hold his state in spight,
Ah cruell chance, ah lucklesse lot, to me poore wretch assign'd,
Was ever seene such contraries, by fraudulent Goddesse blind,
To any one save onely I, imparted for to be,
To amate the mind of any man, did ever *Fortune* she,
Showe forth her selfe so cruell bent, as thus to keepe me backe,
From pointed place by weather driven, my sorrowes more to sacke.
                                                              (ll. 760-767)

Similarly, Clamydes blames his lot on Fortune:

Clamydes ah by fortune she, what froward luck and fate
Most cruelly assigned is, unto thy noble state.
. . .
And shall I be found a faithless Knight, fye on fell fortune she,
Which hath her wheele of froward chance, thus whirled back on me.
. . .
Ah hatefull hap, what shall I say, I see the gods hath signed
Through cruelty my carefull corps, in prison to be pined.
                                                   (ll. 878-893 *passim.*)

Further quotation would show that each knight is concerned about the same thing – the loss of honor to be effected by such miserable circumstances.

Implicit in the stereotyped, generalized expression of theme and human emotion is the rhetorical style which characterizes the play – the series of set speeches, monologues, in which the characters bemoan the vagaries of fortune, extol the glories of war, describe the urgency of love, and the like. In fact, the play is constructed largely in rhetorical rather than dramatic units. Nine of its twenty-three scenes are given over almost entirely to exposition. Of the scenes that advance the action, most have formal settings in which the characters have an opportunity to debate or declaim and only three are truly dramatic (Clyomon's usurpation of Clamydes' place in the knighting ceremony, Clyomon's combat with Thrasellus and Alexander's judgment of the dispute between Mustantius and the Queen of the Strange Marshes). As a rule action is minimized; it is described in report or formalized by the exchange of set speeches – among them, seven formal laments,[5] occasional speeches on the duties of knighthood (ll. 231-241) and on the glories of war (ll. 167-182) and conquest (ll. 360-381), one formal counsel speech (ll. 384-401) and another – Neronis' wooing speech in sc. xii – which represents the variety Clemen calls the "conversion" speech.[6]

The rhetoric of the speeches is uniformly stylized and formal, and the playwright's abundant use of the more common rhetorical devices (rhetorical question, exclamation, apostrophe, interjection and repetition) as well as some less common ones (anaphora, certain auricular devices and the device of "rabbating") suggests a conscious aiming toward the high or elevated style. Thus the play bristles with the high-flown turn of phrase: "Ah cruell grudge that greeves my ghost", "O *Mars* I lawd thy sacred name", and the like. Thus the endless apostrophes and interjections –

---

[5]   On the formal lament in early Renaissance drama see Wolfgang Clemen, *English Tragedy Before Shakespeare*, trans. T. S. Dorsch (London, 1961), pp. 226-255; Robert Y. Turner, "Pathos and the *Gorboduc* Tradition", *HLQ*, XXV (1962), 97-120.

[6]   Clemen, *op. cit.*, pp. 51-55. Clemen classifies the set-speeches in early Renaissance drama as expository, conversion, counsel, occasional, tribunal and emotional.

"Ah wofull sight", "Ah heavens", "Ah death" – the cumbersome
repetitions and circumlocutions that make up the play's style –
near parody, Pistolese, for a modern reader but high seriousness
for its author. Clyomon's lament in the forest after he has done
battle with the King of Norway, killing his adversary but receiving
"greevous wounds" himself, is typical:

Ah my *Neronis* where art thou? ah where art thou become?
For thy sweete sake thy Knight shall here receive his vitall doome.
Lo here all gorde in bloud thy faithfull Knight doth lye,
For thee, ah faithfull dame, thy Knight for lack of help shall dye
For thee, ah here thy *Clyomon*, his mortall stroke hath tane,
For thee, ah these same hands of his, the *Norway* king hath slaine.
Ah bleeding wounds from longer talke my foltring tong doth stay,
And if I have not speedy help, my life doth wast away.

(ll. 1383-1390)

Sometimes the playwright marks the juncture between generalized description of an emotion and its application to the situation
at hand by means of obvious transitions. Thus the King of Norway describes the steadfastness of the lover in general terms:

Where deepe desire hath taken roote, my Lords alas you see,
How that perswasion booteth not, if contrarie it be
Unto the first expected hope, where fancie hath take place,
And vaine it is for to withdraw, by counsell in that case:
The mind who with affection is, to one onely thing affected,
The which may not till dint of death, from them be sure rejected:

(ll. 1121-26)

And having described the general experience, he points its per-
sonal application:

You know my Lords through fame, what force of love hath taken
    place,
Within my breast as touching now *Neronis* noble grace.

(ll. 1127-28)

Neronis' lament in the forest opens similarly with a general description of the pains of unrequited love in terms of the withering
tree and vine and the weed-choked plant. The application to her
own situation is marked by the abrupt transition, "*Neronis*, ah I
am the Tree . . . *Neronis*, ah I am the vine. . . ." At other times

the playwright prefaces these set-speeches with a simile. Thus Neronis:

As Hare the Hound, as Lambe the wolfe, as foule the Fawcons dint,
So do I flie from tyrant he. . . .

Or he may embellish the passage with extended metaphor, as in Bryan's monologue in sc. xxi:

Even as the Owle that hides her head, in hollow tree till night,
And dares not while sir *Phoebus* shines, attempt abroad in flight:
So likewise I as Buzzard bold, while chearefull day is seene,
Am forst with Owle to hide my selfe, amongst the Ivie greene:
And dares not with the seelie Snaile, from cabbin show my head,
Till *Vesper* I behold aloft, in skies begin to spread:
And then as Owle that flies abroad when other fowles do rest,
I creepe out of my drowsie denne, when *Somnus* hath supprest
The head of everie valiant heart, loe thus I shrowd the day,
And travell as the Owle by night upon my wished way:
(ll. 1651-1660)

Lest the point be lost, the playwright invariably explains his metaphors, following the device that Puttenham in his discussion of allegory calls "mixt bicause he [the writer] discouers withall what . . . [his figures] are, which in a full allegorie should not be discouered. . . ." [7]

Such, then, is the artistic mode which the playwright found embodied in his narrative source and which he attempted to transfer to dramatic form. Yet the process of transference was frought with difficulties. Most obvious was the problem of structure, and here it is instructive to remember how he telescoped the abundant action of his source material, particularly the Clamydes-Juliana plot, and how he reduced three principal episodes to two, united these two by the motif of the enmity between the two knights, and constructed both around one simple plot line – love, interference by a villain and the resulting separation of the lovers, and reunion. The two love plots he welded and balanced, moreover, according to the principle of symmetrical construction, which serves as an effective means of conveying order to the

[7]   George Puttenham, *The Arte of English Poesie*, vol. 7 in *English Reprints*, ed. Edward Arber (Birmingham, 1869), p. 198.

abundant action and episodic structure of the romance material. Again comparison with the source is instructive, indicating that he compressed two figures – Harban and Bruyant – into one, retained the figure of Alexander from an earlier portion of the romance, and added Shift and Corin, with the result that the character groupings of the two plots are perfectly symmetrical.[8]

Aside from the symmetrical grouping of characters and the balancing of the two love plots, the structure of the play is governed by the exigency of dramatizing those high points from the romance – wooing scenes, the scene initiating the enmity between the two knights, the scenes in which the knights confront the villains – which could be shown on the stage. Much of the action – for example the slaying of the flying serpent, the kidnapping of Neronis – does not lend itself to the stage. Thus the play is constructed of the rhetorical units devoted to exposition and declamation whose salient features have been noted already. Formal structure, particularly the five-act structure as it had been formulated by the commentators on Terence, is lacking; for unlike plays governed by the requirements of a central conflict and crisis, this play is composed of a series of incidents whose dramatic conflicts may be resolved at practically any given point in the story.

In his handling of the other major problem inherent in the transformation of prose narrative into poetic drama, the playwright was unsuccessful, for he fails to create a poetic medium capable of creating and sustaining a tone suitable to his material. Instead, following the convention formulated in the 1560's,[9] he alternates verse forms so that the low characters usually speak in a doggerel which contrasts strikingly with the regular fourteener couplets that are normal for the play. The fourteeners, usually embellished with alliteration and often with internal rhyme, are relieved by occasional dimeter and tetrameter couplets,[10] anapests (ll. 1633-1648), eight-foot iambic couplets,[11] and once by a lyric in two sixain stanzas in iambic tetrameter (ll. 991-1001).

[8]   See Introduction, pp. 44-45.
[9]   R. W. Bond, *Early Plays from the Italian* (Oxford, 1911), pp. lxxxii-xc.
[10]   ll. 498-500, 751-52, 791-92, 1090-95, 1632-35, 1770-71, 1837-38, 1912-13, 1916-17, 1921-22, 1931-32, 2005-06, 2179-80, 2191-92.
[11]   ll. 372-73, 413-14, 492-93, 2148-2214.

If the general unwieldiness of the versification obscures the author's attempts to vary, adorn, and relieve its regular pattern, one should perhaps remember that the unsuitability of the fourteener and related meters grew in proportion with the Latinizing of the vocabulary and that the anonymous author of *Clyomon and Clamydes* was not alone in his failure to recognize its weakness.[12] One need only be reminded of the popularity of the fourteener from the 'fifties onward – its use in Sternhold and Hopkins' metrical versions of the psalms, in the lyrics of Googe, Turberville, and Howell among others, and in translations of the classics – Phaer's *Virgil* (1558), Golding's *Ovid* (1565-67), Hall's *Iliad* (begun c. 1563-4), and the translations of Seneca (1559-81). The fourteener and its companion form, poulter's measure, reflect the desire for absolute regularity and distinguished English poetry for about twenty years after the publication of Tottel's *Miscellany*.[13] The deficiencies of these forms, only gradually to be recognized, lay in their virtues – the rigid regularity that had brought order to the chaos of early renaissance verse. For it was this order – the unrelieved iambic pattern and the regular placement of the caesura – which forced the distortions of normal syntax noticeable in *Clyomon and Clamydes* – and in the fourteeners of *Patient Grissel, Apius and Virginia, Damon and Pithias*, and most of the drama of the sixties and seventies for that matter – and which produced ultimately, instead of tension between the order of the language and the order of a poetic meter based on that language, a tension between language and a form frought with artificiality.

Following acceptable dramaturgic and poetic practice, then, the author of *Clyomon and Clamydes* uses a metrical pattern which is largely responsible for the incongruities of tone and emphasis which mar the play. Only rarely does he seem aware of the relation between language and the artifice of meter which produces poetry, for he uses his measure indiscriminately, destroying the contrasts in tone that should characterize the voices of his characters and should

---

[12] T. S. Eliot, introduction, *Seneca His Tenne Tragedies* (London, 1927), I, 1-11.
[13] John Thompson, *The Founding of English Metre* (New York, 1961), pp. 15-69.

distinguish their varying moods from the "narrative" portions of the play.

The playwright does not address himself to other problems which the romance material posed – for example, the absence of characterization, the intrusion of evil, which is necessary to the plot but which threatens the tragicomic balance. Instead of adapting, he transfers his source material to dramatic form, retaining much of the artistic mode that characterizes the romance, a mode which fossilizes simplified ideals of human nature and conduct, and depicting these in terms of the conventional and stereotyped in character and action.

c. *Significance*

Enough has been said of the style and content of *Clyomon and Clamydes* to indicate that its significance is extrinsic rather than intrinsic. It is a significance that consists of its literary relationships and, more specifically, its place in the poetic and structural development of English drama from craft to art. There are, for instance, the important relationships that the play bears to its source and the more incidental relationships of details like Neronis' lament (ll. 901-1001) to *The Paradise of Dainty Devices* and Bryan Sans Foy to Spenser's character of that name. There are the foreshadowings of later characters in Corin and Neronis, whose outlines are just barely visible in *As You Like It* [14] and *Cymbeline*, and in Rumor, whose expository function is comparable to Rumor's function in *2 Henry IV*. And there are the more significant developments such as the double love plot, the disguised heroine and the romantic irony implicit in her role, and the secularized Vice. Though one can do no more than speculate, it is probable that this play reflects a fairly typical use of a popular idiom that was to flower later in the hands of genius. The directions the idiom was to take were two: romantic comedy, where its idealisms, improbabilities, and artificialities are juxtaposed with the real or

[14]   For the suggestion that Shakespeare took from Corin the outlines of the rustics in *As You Like It*, see Geoffrey Bullough, *Narrative and Dramatic Sources of Shakespeare* (London, 1958), II, 155-157.

natural in human nature to produce comic incongruity; and dramatic romance, where the same idealisms, improbabilities and artificialities are heightened poetically to produce tragicomic balance and "imaginative congruity".[15] Though *Clyomon and Clamydes* (and *Common Conditions* and *Love and Fortune*, for that matter) accomplishes neither, it supplies the stuff out of which such drama was yet to come.

[15] The term is from Sir Arthur Quiller-Couch, *Shakespeare's Workmanship* (Oxford, 1918), pp. 259-281.

THE
HISTORIE OF
the two valiant Knights,

Syr *Clyomon* Knight of the Golden
Sheeld, sonne to the King of
Denmarke:

And Clamydes *the white Knight, sonne to the*
King of Suauia.

As it hath bene sundry times Acted by her
Maiesties Players.

LONDON

Printed by Thomas Creede.

1599.

CLYOMON AND CLAMYDES

THE CHARACTERS

The King of Swavia
Clamydes, *Son to the King of Swavia*
The King of Denmark
Clyomon, *Son to the King of Denmark*
Alexander the Great
Thrasellus, *King of Norway*
Mustantius, *Brother to the King of the Strange Marshes*
Subtle Shift (Knowledge), *The Vice*
Corin, *A Shepherd*
Bryan Sans Foy, *An Enchanter*
Queen of Denmark
Juliana, *Daughter to the Queen and King of Denmark*
Queen of the Strange Marshes
Neronis, *Daughter to the Queen of the Strange Marshes*

Lords
Heralds
Soldiers   mute
Servants

Boatswain
Ladies
Knights
Page

Rumor
Providence
Corin's dog

THE PROLOGUE

As lately lifting up the leaves of worthy writers workes   [*sig. A2v*]
Wherein the Noble acts and deeds of many hidden lurks,
Our Author he hath found the Glasse of glory shining bright,
Wherein their lives are to be seene, which honour did delight,   5
To be a Lanthorne unto those which dayly do desire,
Apollos Garland by desert, in time for to aspire,
Wherein the froward chances oft, of Fortune you shall see,
Wherein the chearefull countenance, of good successes bee:
Wherein true Lovers findeth joy, with hugie heapes of care,   10
Wherein as well as famous facts, ignomius placed are:
Wherein the just reward of both, is manifestly showne,
That vertue from the roote of vice, might openly be knowne.
And doubting nought right Courteous all, in your accustomed
    woont
And gentle eares, our Author he, is prest to bide the brunt   15
Of bablers tongues, to whom he thinks, as frustrate all his toile,
As peereles caste to filthy Swine, which in the mire doth moile.
Well, what he hath done for your delight, he gave not me in charge,
The Actors come, who shall expresse the same to you at large.

17   caste] Bullen; taste Q

CLYOMON AND CLAMYDES

[i]

Enter Clamydes

Clamydes. As to the wearie wandring wights, whom waltring
   waves environ,
No greater joy of joyes may be, then when from out the Ocean
They may behold the Altitude of Billowes to abate,
For to observe the Longitude of Seas in former rate: 5
And having then the latitude of Sea-roome for to passe,
Their joy is greater through the griefe, then erst before it waȝ.
So likewise I *Clamydes*, Prince of *Swavia* Noble soyle,
Bringing my Barke to *Denmarke* here, to bide the bitter broyle:
And beating blowes of Billowes high, while raging stormes did last,   10
My griefes was greater then might be, but tempests overpast,
Such gentle calmes ensued hath, as makes my joyes more
Through terror of the former feare, then erst it was before.
So that I sit in safetie, as Sea-man under shrowdes,
When he perceives the stormes be past, through vanishing of
   Clowdes.   15
For why, the doubtfull care that drave me off, in daunger to
   prevaile,
Is dasht through bearing lesser braine, and keeping under saile:
So that I have through travell long, at last possest the place
Whereas my Barke in harbour safe, doth pleasures great embrace:
And hath such license limited, as heart can seeme to aske,   20
To go and come of custome free, or any other taske.   [*sig. A3v*]

15   vanishing] Dyce; vanquishing Q

I meane by *Juliana* she, that blaze of bewties breeding,
And for her noble gifts of grace, all other dames exceeding:
Shee hath from bondage set me free, and freed, yet still bound
To her, above all other Dames that lives upon the ground: 25
For had not she bene mercifull, my ship had rusht on Rocks,
And so decayed amids the stormes, through force of clubbish
    knocks:
But when she saw the daunger great, where subject I did stand,
In bringing of my silly Barke, full fraught from out my land,
She like a meeke and modest Dame, what should I else say more?   30
Did me permit with full consent, to land upon her shore:
Upon true promise that I would, here faithfull still remaine,
And that performe which she had vowed, for those that should
    obtaine
Her princely person to possesse, which thing to know I stay,
And then adventurously for her, to passe upon my way.   35
Loe where she comes, ah peereles Dame, my *Juliana* deare.

Enter Juliana *with a white Sheeld.*

Juliana. My *Clamydes*, of troth Sir Prince, to make you stay
    thus here,
I profer too much injurie, thats doubtlesse on my part,
But let it no occasion give, to breede within your hart   40
Mistrust that I should forge or faine, with you my Love in ought.
    Clamydes. No Lady, touching you, in me doth lodge no such
    a thought,
But thankes for your great curtesie that would so friendly heere
In mids of miserie receive, a forraine straunger meere:
But Lady say, what is your will, that it I may perstand?   45
    Juliana. Sir Prince, upon a vow, who spowseth me, must
    needsly take in hand
The flying Serpent for to sley, which in the Forrest is,
That of strange marvels beareth name, which Serpent doth not mis
By dayly use from every coast, that is adjacent there,
To fetch a Virgin maide or wife, or else some Lady faire,   50
To feede his hungrie panch withall, if case he can them take.

His nature loe it onely is, of women spoyle to make:
Which thing no doubt, did daunt me much, and made me vow
   indeed,
Who should espouse me for his wife, should bring to me his head:
Whereto my father willingly, did give his like consent.   55
Lo Sir *Clamydes*, now you know what is my whole intent:
And if you will as I have said, for me this travell take,
That I am yours with heart and mind, your full account do
   make.   [*sig. A4*]
   Clamydes. Ah Lady, if case these travels should surmount, the
   travels whereby came
Unto the worthies of the world, such noble brute and fame,   60
Yea though the dangers should surpasse stout *Hercules* his toyle,
Who fearing nought the dogged feend, sterne *Serbarus* did foyle.
Take here my hand, if life and limbe the living Gods do lend,
To purchase thee, the dearest drop of bloud my heart shall spend.
And therefore Lady lincke with me, thy loyall heart for aye,   65
For I am thine til fates untwine, of vital life the stay:
Protesting here if Gods assist, the Serpent for to kil.
   Juliana. Then shalt thou of all women win, the heart and
   great good wil,
And me possesse for spowsed wife, who in election am
To have the Crowne of *Denmarke* here, as heire unto the same: 70
For why, no children hath my sire besides mee, but one other,
And he indeed is heire before, for that he is my brother.
And *Clyomon* so hight his name, but where he doth remaine,
Unto my Parents is unknowne, for once he did obtaine
Their good wills for to go abroad, a while to spend his daies,   75
In purchasing through active deeds, both honour, laud and
   praise,
Whereby he might deserve to have the order of a Knight:
But this omitting unto thee, *Clamydes* here I plight
My faith and troth, if what is said by me thou dost performe.
   Clamydes. If not, be sure O Lady with my life, I never will
   returne.   80
   Juliana. Then as thou seemest in thine attire, a Virgin Knight
   to be,

Take thou this Sheeld likewise of white, and beare thy name by me,
The white Knight of the Silver Sheeld, to elevate thy praise.
Clamydes. O Lady as your pleasure is, I shall at all assayes
Endevour thy good will to win, if *Mars* do send me might,   85
Such honour as your grace with joy, shall welcome home your
    Knight.
Juliana. Then farewell my deare *Clamydes*, the gods direct
    thy way,
And graunt that with the Serpents head, behold thy face I may.
Clamydes. You shall not need to doubt thereof, O faithfull-
Dame so true,
And humbly kissing here thy hand, I bid thy Grace adue.   90

Exit [Juliana].

Ah happie time and blisfull day, wherein by fate I find
Such friendly favours as is foode, to feede both heart and mind:
To *Suavia* soile I swiftly will prepare my foot-steps right, [*sig. A4v*]
There of my father to receive the order of a Knight: 95
And afterwards addresse my selfe in hope of honours Crowne,
Both Tyger fell and Monster fierce, by dint for to drive downe.
The flying Serpent soone shall feele, how boldly I dare vaunt me,
And if that *Hydras* head he had, yet dread should never daunt me.
If murdering *Minataure*, a man might count this ougly beast,   100
Yet for to win a Lady such, I do account it least
Of travels toyle to take in hand, and therefore farewell care,
For hope of honour sends me forth, mongst warlike wights to
    share.
Exit.

[ii]

Enter Sir Clyomon *Knight of the golden Sheeld, sonne to the*   105
    King of Denmarke, *with subtill* Shift *the Vice, booted.*
Clyomon. Come on good fellow follow me, that I may understand

81   Virgin] Bullen; Virgins Q
85   thy] my Q
91   *Exit.*] Bullen; l. 89 in Q

Of whence thou art, thus travelling here in a forraine land:
Come why dost thou not leave loytering there, and follow after me?
   Shift [within]. Ah I am in ant shall please you. 110
   Clyomon. In, why where art thou in?
   Shift [within]. Faith in a dirtie Ditch with a woman, so beraide,
as it's pittie to see.
   Clyomon. Wel, I see thou art a merrie companion, I shall like
better of thy company:
But I pray thee come away.
   Shift [within]. If I get out one of my legs as fast as I may 115
Ha lo, A my buttocke, the very foundation thereof doth breake:
Ha lo, once againe, I am as fast, as though I had frozen here a
weeke.
   Here let him slip on to the Stage backwards, as though he had
   puld his leg out of the mire, one boote off, and rise up to run
   in againe. 120
   Clyomon. Why how now, whither runst thou, art thou foolish
in thy mind?
   Shift. But to fetch one of my legs ant shall please, that I have
left in the mire behind.
   Clyomon. One of thy legs, why looke man, both thy legs thou
hast,
It is but one of thy bootes thou hast lost, thy labour thou doest
wast. 125
   Shift. But one of my bootes? Jesu, I had such a wrench with
the fall,
That I assure, I did thinke one of my legs had gone withall.
   Clyomon. Well let that passe, and tell me what thou art, and
what is thy name?
And from whence thou cam'st, and whither thy journey thou
doest frame,
That I have met thee by the way, thus travelling in this sort? 130
                                          [*sig. B1*]
   Shift. What you have requested, ant shall please, I am able
to report,   *B1*

118   *on to*] *unto* Q

What I am by my nature each wight shall perceive
That frequenteth my company, by the learning I have.
I am the sonne of *Appollo*, and from his high seate I came,
But whither I go, it skils not, for Knowledge is my name: 135
And who so hath knowledge, what needs he to care
Which way the wind blowe, his way to prepare.
   Clyomon. And art thou Knowledge? of troth I am glad that
I have met with thee.
   Shift. I am Knowledge, and have as good skill in a woman
as any man whatsoever he bee. 140
For this I am certaine of, let me but lie with her all night,
And Ile tell you in the morning, whither she is maide, wife, or
spright:
And as for other matters, speaking of languishes, or any other
thing,
I am able to serve ant shall please, ant were great *Alexander*
the King.
   Clyomon. Of troth, then for thy excellencie, I will thee
gladly entertaine, 145
If in case that with me thou wilt promise to remaine.
   Shift. Nay ant shall please ye, I am like to a woman, say nay
and take it,
When a gentleman profers entertainment, I were a foole to for-
sake it.
   Clyomon. Well Knowledge, then sith thou art content my
servant to bee,
And endued with noble qualities, thy personage I see, 150
Thou having perfect knowledge, how thy selfe to behave:
I will send thee of mine arrant, but haste thither I crave:
For here I will stay thy comming againe.
   Shift. Declare your pleasure sir, and whither I shall go, and
then the case is plaine. 155
   Clyomon. Nay of no great importance, but being here in
Suavia
And neare unto the Court, I would have thee to take thy way
Thither with all speede, because I would heare

If any shewes or triumphs be towards, else would I not come
there,
For onely upon feates of armes, is all my delight.   160
  Shift. If I had knowne so much before, serve that serve will,
I would have serv'd no martiall Knight.   [*Aside.*]
Well sir, to accomplish your will, to the court I will hy,
And what newes is there stirring, bring word by and by.

                    Exit.   165

  Clyomon. Do so good Knowledge, and here in place thy com-
ming I will stay,   [*sig. B1v*]
For nothing doth delight me more, then to heare of martiall
play:
Can foode unto the hungrie corps, be cause of greater joy,
Then for the haughtie heart to heare, which doth it selfe imploy,
Through martiall excercises much to winne the brute of Fame,   170
Where mates do meete which thereunto their fancies seemes to
frame:
Can musicke more the pensive heart or daunted mind delight,
Can comfort more the carefull corps and overpalled spright,
Rejoyce, then sound of Trumpet doth each warlike wight allure,
And Drum and Fyfe unto the fight doth noble hearts procure,   175
To see in sunder shivered, the Lance that leades the way,
And worthy knights unbeavered, in field amidst the fray,
To heare the ratling Cannons roare, and Hylts on Helmets ring,
To see the souldiers swarme on heapes, where valiant hearts doth
bring
The cowardly crew into the case of carefull Captives band,   180
There aunciers brave displayed be, and wonne by force of hand.
What wight would not as well delight as this to heare and see,
Betake himselfe in like affaires a fellow mate to bee,
With *Clyomon*, to *Denmarke* King the onely sonne and heire
Who of the Golden Sheeld as now, the knightly name doth beare   185
In every land since that I foyld the worthy Knight of Fame,
Sir *Samuel* before the King, and Prince of martiall game,
Alexander cald the Great, which when he did behold,

He gave to me in recompence, this Shield of glittering Gold:
Requesting for to know my name, the which shall not be showen 190
To any Knight, unlesse by force he make it to be knowen,
For so I vowed to *Denmarke* King, my fathers grace when I
First got his leave, that I abroad my force and strength might
  try.
And so I have my selfe behav'd, in Citie, Towne and field,
That never yet did fall reproach, to the Knight of the Golden
  Shield. 195

Enter Subtill Shift, *running.*

Shift. Gods ames, where are you, where are you? and you bee
a man come away.
  Clyomon. Why what is the matter Knowledge? to tell thy
  arrand stay.
  Shift. Stay, what talke you of staying, why then all the sight
  will be past, 200
Clamides the Kings sonne shall be dubd Knight in all hast.
  Clyomon. Ah Knowledge, then come indeed, and good
  pastime thou shalt see,
For I will take the honour from him that dubbed I may bee [*sig. B2*].
Upon a couragious stomacke, come let us haste thither.

Exit. 205

  Shift. Leade you the way and ile follow, weele be both made
  knights togither,
Ah sirrah, is my maister so lustie, or dares he be so bold?
It is no marvell then, if he beare a Sheeld of Gold.
But by your patience if he continue in this businesse, farewell
  maister than,
For I promise you, I entend not very long to be his man: 210
Although under the tytle of Knowledge my name I do faine,
Subtill Shift I am called, that is most plaine.
And as it is my name, so it is my nature also,
To play the shifting knave wheresoever I go.
Well, after him I will, but soft now, if my maister chance to be
  lost 215

And any man examine me, in telling his name I am as wise as a
post.
What a villaine was I, that ere he went, could not aske it?
Well, its no great matter, I am but halfe bound, I may serve
whom I will yet.

Exit.

[iii]

Enter the King of Suavia, *with the Herauld before*   220
him: Clamydes, *three Lords.*

King. Come *Clamides,* thou our sonne, thy Fathers talke attend,
Since thou art prest thy youthfull dayes in prowesse for to spend:
And doest of us the order aske, of knighthood for to have,
We know thy deeds deserves the same, and that which thou doest
     crave   225
Thou shalt possesse: but first my sonne, know thou thy fathers
     charge,
And what to knighthood doth belong, thine honour to enlarge:
Unto what end a knight is made, that likewise thou maiste know,
And beare the same in mind also, that honour thine may flow
Amongst the worthies of the world, to thy immortall fame: 230
Know thou therefore, *Clamydes* deare, to have a knightly name
Is first above all other things his God for to adore,
In truth according to the lawes prescribde to him before.
Secondly, that he be true unto his Lord and king.
Thirdly, that he keepe his faith and troth in every thing.   235
And then before all other things that else we can commend,
That he be alwaies ready prest, his countrey to defend:
The Widow, poore, and fatherlesse, or Innocent bearing blame,
To see their cause redressed right, a faithfull knight must frame: 239
                    [*sig. B2v*]
In truth he alwaies must be tried, this is the totall charge,
That will receive a knightly name, his honour to enlarge.
     Clamydes. O Father, this your gracious counsell given, to me
your onely sonne,

Shall not be in oblivion cast, till vitall race be runne:
What way dooth winne Dame Honours Crowne, those pathes my
steppes shall trace, 245
And those that to reproach doth leade, which seeketh to deface
True Honour in her Regall seate, I shall detest for aye,
And be as utter enemie, to them both night and day:
By flying force of flickring fame, your grace shall understand
Of my behaviour noble syre, in every forraine land. 250
And if you heare by true report, I venture in the Barge
Of wilfulnesse contrary this, your graces noble charge:
Let ignomie to my reproach, in steed of Lady fame,
Sound through the earth and Azure Skies, the strained blast of
shame:
Whereby within Oblivions Tombe, my deeds shall de detained, 255
Where otherwise of memorie, the mind I might have gained:
So that the den of darksomenesse, shall ever be my chest,
Where worthy deeds prefers each wight, with honour to be blest.
    King. Well *Clamydes* then kneele downe, according as is
right,
That here thou mayst receive of me, the order of a Knight. 260
    Here let him kneele downe, Clyomon *with subtill* Shift *watching
in place, and as the King doth go about to lay the Mace of his
head, let* Clyomon *take the blowe, and so passe away presently.*
    Shift. Now prepare your selfe, or ile be either a Knight or a
knave.
    Clyomon. Content thy selfe Knowledge, for ile quickly him
deceive. 265
    King. The Noble order of a Knight, *Clamydes* unto thee
We give through due desert, wherefore see that thou bee,
Both Valiant, Wise, and Hardie.
    Shift. Away now quickly, least we be take tardie.

                 Exeunt [Clyomon *and* Shift.] 270

    King. Ah stout attempt of Barron bold, that hath from this
my sonne,

266   order] Dyce; orders Q

The Knight-hood tane, my Lords pursue, ere far he can be runne.

[Two Lords] *Pursue him.* [*sig. B3*]

Ah *Clamydes* how art thou bereft of honour here?
Was like presumption ever seene, that one a straunger meere, 27£
Should come in presence of a Prince, and tempt as he hath done,
To take the Knight-hood thus away, from him who is his sonne?
  Clamydes. Ah father, how am I perplext, till I revenged be,
Upon the wretch which here hath tane, the honour thus from me?
Was ever any one deceiv'd of Knight-hood so before? 28C
  King. Well *Clamydes*, my Lords return, stay till we do know
more.

Enter Shift *brought in by the two Lords, who*
pursued Clyomon.

  1. Lord. O King the knight is fled and gone, pursute prevail-
eth nought.
But here his slave we taken have, to tell why this he wrought. 285
  King. Ah cruell grudge that greeves my ghost, shall he escape
me so?
Shall he with honour from my sonne, without disturbance go?
Ah Catiffe thou, declare his name, and why he ventred here:
Or death shall be thy guerdon sure, by all the Gods I sweare.
  Shift. Ah ant shall please you, I know neither him, his country
nor name. 290
  2. Lord. What, what sir, are not you his servant? will you
denie the same?
  King. Nay then you are a dissembling knave, I know very
well.
  Shift. Ant shall please your Grace, even the very troth I shall
tell,
I should have bene his servant when we met togither,
Which was not full three houres before we came hither. 295
  King. Well what is his name, and of what countrey declare?

273 *Pursue him.*] *Pursue him, and bring in* Shift. Q

Shift. That cannot I tell ant shall please you, you never saw
servant in such care,
To know his Maisters name: neither in Towne nor Field,
And what he was he would tell, but the Knight of the Golden
    Sheeld. 300
    King. Well, *Clamydes* marke my charge, what I to thee shall say,
Prepare thy selfe for to pursue that Traytor on his way:
Which hath thine honour reft from thee, and either by force of
    hand
Or love, his name and native soyle, see that thou understand,
That I may know for what intent, he bare this grudge to thee, 305
Else see thou never doest returne againe to visit mee:
For this imports him for to be, of valiant heart and mind:
And therefore do pursue thy foe, untill thou doest him find,
                         [*sig. B3v*]
To know his name and what he is, or as I said before,
Do never view thy father I, in presence any more. 310
    Clamydes. Well father, sith it is your charge, and precept
    given to mee,
And more for mine owne honours sake, I franckly do agree
To undertake the enterprise, his name to understand,
Or never else to shew my face againe in *Swavia* land.
Wherefore I humbly do desire, the order to receive, 315
Of Knighthood, which my sole desire hath ever bene to have:
It is the name and meane, whereby true honour is atchived,
Let me not then O father deare, thereof be now deprived:
Sith that mine honour cowardly was stolne by Caitiffe he,
And not by dinted dastards deed, O father lost by me. 320
    King. Well *Clamides*, then kneele downe, here in our Nobles
    sight,
We give to thee that art our sonne, the order of a Knight:
But as thou wilt our favour winne, accomplish my desire.
    Clamydes. Else never to your royall Court, O father ile retire.
    King. Well, then adue *Clamides* deare, the Gods thine ayder be: 325
But come my Lords, to have his hire, that Caitiffe bring with me.
    Shift. Alas ant shall please you, I am Knowledge, and no evill
    did pretend,

Set me at libertie, it was the knight that did offend.

Clamydes.   O father, sith that he is Knowledge, I beseech your
grace set him free,

For in these affaires, he shall waite and tend on mee: 330

If he will protest, to be true to me ever.

Shift.   Ah Noble *Clamydes*, heeres my hand, ile deceive you
never.

Clamydes.   Wel then father, I beseech your Grace grant that I
may have him.

King.   Well *Clamydes*, I am content, sith thou my sonne doest
crave him.

Receive him therefore at my hands. My Lords come lets depart.

Omnes.   We ready are to waite on you O King, with willing
hart.   336

Exeunt.

Clamydes.   Well Knowledge, do prepare thy selfe, for here I
do protest,

My fathers precepts to fulfill, no day nor night to rest

From toylsome travell, till I have revengd my cause aright,   340

On him who of the golden Sheeld, now beareth name of knight:

Who of mine honour hath me robd, in such a cowardly sort,

As for to be of noble heart, it doth him not import.

But Knowledge, to me thy service still thou must with loyall hart
professe.   [*sig. B4*]

Shift.   Use me that all other villains may take ensample by me,
if I digresse.   345

Clamydes.   Well then come follow speedily, that him pursue
we may.

Exit.   346b

Shift.   Keepe you before ant shall please you, for I mind not
to stay.

Ah sirrah *Shift*, thou wast driven to thy shifts now indeed,

I dreamed before, that untowardly I should speed:

And yet it is better lucke then I looked to have: 350

But as the proverbe saith, good fortune ever hapneth to the veryest
knave:

And yet I could not escape with my maister, do what I can,
Well by this bargaine he hath lost his new Serving-man:
But if *Clamydes* overtake him now, what buffets will there be,
Unlesse it be foure miles off the fray, there will be no standing for
  me.   355
Well after him I will, but howsoever my maister speed,
To shift for my selfe I am fully decreed.

Exit.   357b

[iv]

Enter King Alexander *the Great, as valiantly set forth as may be,
and as many soldiers as can.*

  Alexander. After many invincible victories, and conquests
    great atchived,   360
I *Alexander* with sound of Fame, in safetie am arrived
Upon my borders long wished for, of *Macedonia* soile,
And all the world subject have, through force of warlike toile.
O *Mars* I lawd thy sacred name, and for this safe returne,
To *Pallas* Temple will I wend, and sacrifices burne   365
To thee, *Bellona* and the rest, that warlike wights do guide,
Who for King *Alexander* did, such good successe provide.
Who bowes not now unto my becke, my force who doth not feare?
Who doth not of my conquests great, throughout the world heare?
What King as to his soveraigne Lord, doth now not bow his knee? 370
What Prince doth raigne upon the earth, which yeelds not unto
  mee
Due homage for his Regall Mace? What countrey is at libertie?
What Dukedome, Iland, or Province else, to me now are not
  tributarie?
What Fort of Force, or Castle strong, have I not battered downe?
What Prince is he, that now by me, his Princely seate and Crowne 375
Doth not acknowledge for to hold? not one the world throughout,
But of King *Alexanders* power they all do stand in doubt:
They feare as Fowles that hovering flie, from out the Fawcons
  way,

As Lambe the Lyon, so my power, the stowtest do obey.
In field who hath not felt my force, where battering blowes
    abound?   [*sig. B4v*]   38(
King or Keysar, who hath not fixt his knees to me on ground?
And yet *Alexander*, what art thou? thou art a mortall wight,
For all that ever thou hast got or wonne by force in fight.
    1. Lord. Acknowledging thy state O King, to be as thou hast
said,
The Gods no doubt as they have bene, will be thy sheeld and aid   38⁵
In all attempts thou takst in hand, if case no glorie vaine
Thou seekest, but acknowledging thy victories and gaine,
Through the providence of sacred Gods to happen unto thee:
For vaine is trust, that in himselfe, man doth repose we see,
And therefore least these victories which thou O King hast got   390
Should blind thine eyes with arrogancie, thy noble fame to blot,
Let that victorious Prince his words, of *Macedon* thy sire,
To acknowledge still thy state O King, thy noble heart inspire,
Who after all his victories, triumphantly obtained,
Least that the great felicitie of that which he had gained,   395
Should cause him to forget himselfe, a child he did provide,
Which came unto his chamber doore, and every morning cryde
Philip, thou art a mortall man: this practise of thy sire,
Amidst all these thy victories, thy servant doth desire,
O *Alexander* that thou wilt, them print within thy mind,   400
And then no doubt as father did, thou solace sweete shall find.
    Alexander. My Lords, your counsell doubtlesse I esteeme, and
with great thanks againe,
I do requite your courtesie, rejecting this is plaine,
All vaine glory from my heart: and since the Gods divine,   405
To us above all other Kings, this fortune doeth assigne,
To have in our subjection the world for most part,
We will at this our home returne, with fervent zeale of hart,
In *Pallas* Temple to the gods, such sacrifices make,
Of thankfulnesse for our successe, as they in part shall take   410

395   he] Dyce; she Q
406   other] Dyce; others Q
408   our home] Bullen; one hour Q

The same, a gratulation, sufficient from us sent:
Come therefore let us homewards march, to accomplish our
   intent.
Omnes. We readie are most famous King, to follow thee with
   victorie.
Alexander. Then sound your drums and Trumpets both, that
we may march triumphantly.   415

                 Exeunt.   [*sig. C1*]

              [v]

    Enter Sir Clyomon, *Knight of G. S.*

Clyomon. Now *Clyomon* a knight thou art, though some per-
   haps may say,
Thou cowardly camst to *Clamydes*, and stole his right away:
No, no, it was no cowardly part, to come in presence of a king,   420
And in the face of all his Court, to do so worthy a thing:
Amidst the mates that martiall be, and sterne knights of his hall,
To take the knighthood from their Prince, even mauger of them
   all.
It gives a guerdon of good will, to make my glory glance,
When warlike wights shall heare thereof, my fame they will
   advance: 425
And where I was pretended late, to *Denmarke* king my sire,
His royal grace to see, homeward to retire,
Now is my purpose altered by brute of late report,
And where fame resteth to be had, thither *Clyomon* will resort:
For as I understand by fame, that worthy Prince of might,   430
The conqueror of conquerors, who *Alexander* hight,
Returning is to *Macedon*, from many bloudie broyle,
And there to keepe his royall Court, now after wearie toyle:
Which makes the mind of *Clyomon*, with joyes to be clad,
For there I know of martiall mates, is company to be had.   435
Adieu therefore, both *Denmarke* king and *Suavia* Prince beside,
To *Alexanders* Court I will, the Gods my journey guide.

Enter Clamydes *and* Shift.

Clamydes. Come Knowledge here he is, nay stay thou cowardly knight,

That like a dastard camst, to steale away my right.   44(

Clyomon. What, what, you raile sir princkocks Prince, me
coward for to call.

Shift. Ant shall please you he is a coward, he would have
hyrde me, amidst your fathers hall,

To have done it for him, being himselfe in such stay

That scarcely he durst, before your presence appeare.   445

Clyomon. Why how now Knowledge, what forsake thy maister
so soone?

Shift. Nay maister was, but not maister is, with you I have
done.

Clamydes. Well for what intent camst thou, my honour to
steale away?

Clyomon. That I tooke ought from thee, I utterly deny.

Clamydes. Didst not thou take the honour, which my father to
me gave?   450

Clyomon. Of that thou hadst not, I could thee not deprave.

Clamydes. Didst not thou take away my knighthood from me?

Clyomon. No, for I had it before it was given unto thee:

[*sig. C1v*]

And having it before thee, what Argument canst thou make

That ever from thee the same I did take?   455

Shift. Thats true, he receiv'd the blow before at you it came,

And therefore he tooke it not from you, because you had not the
same.

Clamydes. Well, what hight thy name, let me that understand,

And wherefore thou travailedst here in my fathers land

So boldly to attempt in his Court such a thing?   460

Clyomon. The bolder attempt is, more fame it doth bring:

But what my name is desirest thou to know?

Shift. Nay he hath stolen sheepe I thinke, for he is ashamd
his name for to show.

443   amidst. . .] Amidst. . . Separate line in Q

Clamydes. What thy name is, I would gladly perstand: 465
Clyomon. Nay that shall never none know, unlesse by force
of hand
He vanquish me in fight, such a vow have I made,
And therefore to combat with me, thy selfe do perswade,
If thou wilt know my name.
    Clamydes. Well, I accord to the same.   470
    Shift. Nay then God be with you, if you be at that poynt I
am gone.
If you be of the fighters disposition, ile leave you alone.
    Clamydes. Why stay Knowledge, although I fight, thou shalt
not be molested.
    Shift. Ant shall please you, this feare hath made me beray my
selfe, with a Proynstone that was not digested.   475

[*Exit.*]

    Clyomon. Well *Clamydes* stay thy selfe, and marke my sayings
here:
And do not thinke I speake this same, for that thy force I feare,
But that more honour may redound, unto the victors part,
Wilt thou here give thy hand to me, withouten fraud of hart
Upon the faith which to a knight doth rightly appertaine,   480
And by the loyaltie of a knight, ile sweare to thee againe,
For to observe my promise just, which is if thou agree,
The fifteenth day next following, to meete Sir Prince with mee,
Before King *Alexanders* grace, in *Macedonia* soyle,
Who all the world subject hath, through force of warlike toyle: 485
For he is chief of chivalrie, and king of Martiall mates,
And to his royall Court thou knowest, repaire all estates.
Give me thy hand upon thy faith, of promise not to faile,
And here is mine to thee againe, if Fortunes froward gaile, [*sig. C2*]
Resist me not, the day forespoke to meete sir Prince with thee,   490
Before that king to try our strengths: say if thou doest agree,
For tryple honour will it be, to him that gets the victorie,
Before so worthy a Prince as hee, and Nobles all so publikely,
Where otherwise if in this place we should attempt the same,
Of the honour that were got thereby, but small would be the fame.   495

Clamydes. Well Sir knight, here is my hand, ile meete in place forespoke.
Clyomon. And by the loyaltie of a knight, ile not my words revoke.
Till then adieu, ile keepe my day.

Exit.

Clamydes. And I, if fates do not gainsay.   500

[*Re-enter* Shift.]

Shift. What is he gone, and did take no leave of me?
Jesu so unmannerly a Gentleman did any man see,
But now my Lord which will you travell declare?
Clamydes. Sith I have fifteene dayes respit my selfe to prepare,
My Ladies charge for to fulfill, behold I do entend.   505
Shift. Your Lady ant shall please you, why who is your Lady,
may a man be so bold as aske and not offend?
Clamydes. *Juliana* daughter to the King of *Denmarke* loe
is she,
Whose knight I am, and from her hands, this shield was given
to me,
In signe and token of good will, whose noble grace to gaine,   510
I have protested in her cause for to omit no paine
Nor travaille, till I have subdued the flying Serpents force,
Which in the forrest of Marvels is, who taketh no remorse
Of womenkind, but doth devoure all such as are a stray,
So that no one dares go abroad, nor wander forth the way.   515
And sith I have yet fifteene dayes, my selfe for to prepare,
To meete the Knight of the Golden Shield, my heart is voyd of
care.
I will unto the Forrest wend, sith it is in my way,
And for my *Julianas* sake, that cruell Serpent slay.
Shift. What are you a mad man, will you wilfully be slaine?   520
If you go into that Forrest, you will never come out againe.

498   ——] *Clamy.* Q

Clamydes. Why so Knowledge, dost thou thinke the Serpent
I feare?

Shift. No, but do you not know of *Bryan sance foy,* the champion dwels there?

Clamydes. A cowardly knight Knowledge is he, and dares
fight with no man.   [*sig. C2v*] 525

Shift. Ah a noble match, couple him and me togither than:
Yea, but although he dares not fight, an Enchanter he is,
And whosoever comes in that Forrest, to enchant he doth not mis

Clamydes. Tush, tush, I feare him not Knowledge, and therefore come away.

                               Exit.   530

Shift. Well seeing you are so wilfull, go you before ile not stay.
Ah sirrah, now I know all my maisters mind, the which I did not
    before,
He adventureth for a Lady, well I say no more:
But to escape the enchantments of *Bryan Sance foy,*
Thats *Bryan* without faith, I have devisde a noble toy: 535
For he and I am both of one consanguinitie,
The veryest cowardly villaine that ever was borne, thats of a
    certaintie.
Ile fight with no man, no more will *Bryan,* thats plaine:
But by his enchantments, he putteth many to great paine.
And in a Forrest of strange marvels doth he keepe,   540
Altogither by enchantments to bring men a sleepe,
Till he have wrought his will of them: to *Bryan* straight will I,
And of my maisters comming to the Forrest informe him privily,
So shall I win his favour, and subtill *Shift* in the end,
Thou shalt escape his enchantment, for he will be thy frend: 545
Well unknowne to my maister, for mine owne safegard this will
    I do,
And now like a subtill shifting knave, after him ile go.

                               Exit.   547b

527   an] Dyce; and Q

[vi]

Enter Bryan sance foy.

Bryan. Of *Brian sance foi* who hath not heard? not for his
valiant acts,
But well I know throughout the world, doth ring his cowardly
facts.   550
What tho I pray, all are not borne to be God *Mars* his men,
To toy with daintie dames in courts, should be no copesmates
then.
If all were given to chivalrie, then *Venus* might go weepe,
For any Court in Venerie, that she were like to keepe.
But shall I frame then mine excuse, by serving *Venus* she,   555
When I am knowne throughout the world, faint hearted for to be?
No, no alas, it will not serve, for many a knight in love,
Most valiant hearts no doubt they have, and knightly prowesse
prove,
To get their Ladies loyall hearts, but I in *Venus* yoke,
Am forst for want of valiancie, my freedome to provoke: 560
Bearing the name and port of knight, enchantments for to use,
[*sig. C3*]
Wherewith full many a worthy wight, most cowardly I abuse:
As witnesseth the number now, which in my Castle lye,
Who if they were at libertie, in armes I durst not try,
The feeblest there though he unarmd, so is my courage danted,   565
When as I see the glittering armes, whereby each Knight is vanted.
But how I vanquish these same Knights, is wonderfull to see,
And Knights that ventured for her love, whom I do love they
bee.
Thats *Juliana*, daughter to the King of *Denmarks* grace,
Whose beautie is the cause that I do haunt or keepe this place.   570
For that no wight may her possesse, unlesse by vow decreed,
He bring and do present to her the flying Serpents head.
Which many hath attempt to do, but none yet could him slay,
Ne afterward hence backe againe, for me could passe away:
For that through my inchantments lo, which heere this forrest
keepe,
                                                                         575
So soone as I did looke on them, they straight were in a sleepe.

Then presently I them unarmd, and to my Castle brought,
And there in prison they do lye, not knowing what was wrought.
Lo thus I range the woods to see who doth the Serpent slay,
That by inchantment I may take the head from him away,   580
And it present unto the Dame, as though I were her Knight:
Well heere comes one, ile shrowd my selfe, for sure I will not
fight.

     Enter Subtill Shift.

 Shift. Gogs bloud where might I meete with that cowardly
knave *Bryan sance foy?*
I could tell him such a tale now as would make his hart leape
 for joy.   585
Well yonder I have espied one, whatsoever he be.
 Bryan. Nay gogs bloud ile be gone, he shall not fight with me,
But by inchantment ile be even with him by and by.
 Shift. A ant shall please you, ile fight with no man, never
come so nye.
 Bryan. Why what art thou declare? whither doost thou run?   590
 Shift. Even the cowardlyest villaine ant shall please you that
lives under the sun.
 Bryan. What of my fraternitie, doest thou not know *Bryan
sance foy?*
 Shift. What maister *Bryan,* Jesu how my hart doth leape for
joy
That I have met with you, who ever had better lucke?
But touch me not.   595
 Bryan. Wherefore?
 Shift. A lest you inchant me into the likenesse of a bucke.
           [*sig. C3v*]
 Bryan. Tush, tush, I warrant thee, but what art thou declare?
 Shift. Knowledge ant shall please you, who hither doth re-
paire
To tell you good newes.   600
 Bryan. Good newes? what are they Knowledge expresse?

595 ——] Dyce; *Bryan* Q   The speech headings through l. 605 alternate
  erroneously in Q and have been emended as necessary.
599 ant] and it Q

Shift. A Knight hath slaine the flying Serpent.

Bryan. Tush it is not so.

Shift. It is most true that I do confesse.

Bryan. Ah what hight his name Knowledge? let me that
understand.   605

Shift. *Clamydes* the White Knight, sonne to the King of
Swavia land,

Who for *Juliana*, daughter to the King of *Denmarks* grace,

Did take the attempt in hand, now you know the whole case.

Bryan. Ah happy newes of gladsomnesse unto my danted
mind,

Now for to winne my Ladyes love, good fortune is assignd: 610

For though she be *Clamydes*, right wonne worthely indeed,

Yet will I sure possesse that Dame, by giving of the head.

But Knowledge where about declare, doeth that Clamydes rest?

Shift. Even hard by in the Forrest heere where he slew the
beast.

I left him, and to seeke you did hye: 615

But let us go furder into the woods, you shall meete him by
and by.

Bryan. Well Knowledge for thy paines take this as some
reward,

And if thou wilt abide with me, be sure ile thee regard

Above all others of my men, besides ile give to thee

A thing, that from inchantments aye, preserved shalt thou be.   620

Shift. Then here is my hand, ile be your servant ever:

Bryan. And seeing thou art a coward as well as I, ile forsake
thee never.

But come let us go *Clamydes* to meete.

Exit.

Shift. Keepe on your way and ile follow, I trust if he meete   625
him, heele take him to his feete.

Gogs bloud was ever seene such a jolt-headed villaine as he,

To be so afraid of such a faint-hart knave as I am to see?

Of the fraternitie quoth you? birlady its a notable brood:

606   *Shift.*] Dyce; ——Q

Well *Shift* these chinks doeth thy hart some good: 630
And ile close with *Bryan* till I have gotten the thing
That he hath promised me, and then ile be with him to bring.
Well, such shifting knaves as I am, the Ambodexter must play,
[*sig. C4*]
And for commoditie serve every man, whatsoever the world say.
Well after *Bryan* I will, and close with him awhile, 635
But as well as *Clamydes*, in the end ile him begile.

[*Exit.*]

[vii]

Enter Clamydes, *with the head upon his sword.*

Clamydes. Ah happy day my deadly foe submitted hath to
death,
Lo heere the hand, lo heere the sword that stopt the vitall
breath:
Lo heere the head that shall possesse my *Juliana* deare, 640
The Knight of the golden Sheeld his force, what neede I now to
feare:
Since I by force subdued have this Serpent fierce of might,
Who vanquisht hath as I have heard, full many a worthie Knight,
Which for to winne my Ladyes love, their lives have venterd
heere.
Besides that cowardly *Bryan* which the faithlesse shield doth
beare, 645
A number keepes as I have heard, as captives in his hold,
Whome he hath by inchantment got, and not through courage
bold.
Shall such defamed dastards, dard by Knights, thus beare their
name?
Shall such as are without all faith, live to impaire our fame?
Shall valiant harts by cowardly charme, be kept in captives
thrall? 650
Shall Knights live subject to a wretch which hath no hart at all?

640 *Juliana*] Dyce; *Julianas* Q

Nay first *Clamydes* claime to thee fell *Atrapos* her stroke,
Ere thou doest see such worthy Knights to bear the heavie yoke,
Of cowardly *Bryan* without faith, his charmes let daunt not thee,
And for his force thou needst not feare, the Gods thy shield
    will be.   655
Well, to meete the Knight of the golden Shield, yet ten daies space
    I have
And to set free these worthy Knights, but rest a while I crave.
Heere in this place neere to this fort, for that I weary am
With travell, since from killing of the Serpent late I came:
Lo heere a while I mind to rest, and *Bryan* then subdue,   660
And then to *Alexanders* court, to keepe my promise true.
    Heere let him sit downe and rest himselfe.   661b

    Enter Bryan sance foy, *and* Shift.

    Bryan. Come Knowledge, for here he lyes layd weary on the
ground:
    Shift. Nay, ile not come in his sight, if you would give me a
thousand pound.
For he is the terriblest Knight of any you have heard spoke,   665
Heele beate a hundreth such as you and I am downe at one
    stroke.
    Bryan. Tush, feare thou naught at all, I have charmed him,
and he is fast asleepe,
Lying neere unto the Castle here which I do keepe.
And ten dayes in this sleepe I have charm'd him to remaine,
                    [*sig. C4v*]
Before nature shall overcome it, that he might wake againe.   670
In the meane season, lo behold the Serpents head ile take away,
His shield and his apparell; this done, then will I convay
His body into prison, with other his companions to lye,
Whose strengths, ah Knowledge, I durst never attempt to try.
    Shift. Ah handle him softly, or else you will cause him to
    awake: 675

652 her] Dyce; his Q
661b *Heere ... himselfe.*] in margin, ll. 659-661 in Q

Bryan. Tush, tush, not if all the noyse in the world I were able
to make:
Till ten dayes be expired, the charme will not leave him,
And then I am sure he will marvell who did thus deceive him:
So now he is stripped, stay thou here for a season,
And ile go fetch two of my servants to cary him into prison. 680

Exit.

Shift. Well do so maister *Bryan*, and for your comming ile
stay,
Gogs bloud what a villaine am I my maister to betray.
Nay sure ile awake him if it be possible ere they carry him to
jayle:
Maister, what maister, awake man, what maister, ah it will not
prevaile. 685
Am not I worthie to be hangd, was ever seene such a deceitfull
knave?
What villany was in me, when unto *Bryan* understanding I gave
Of my maisters being in this forrest, but much I muse indeed
What he meanes to do with my maisters apparell, his shield and
the head?
Well, seeing it is through my villany, my maister is at this drift, 690
Yet when he is in prison, *Shift* shall not be voide of a shift
To get him away, but if it ever come to his eare
That I was the occasion of it, heele hang me thats cleare.
Well heere comes *Bryan*, ile cloke with him if I may,
To have the keeping of my maister in prison night and day. 695

Enter Bryan sance foy, *two servants.*

Bryan. Come sirs take up this body, and cary it into the appointed place,
And there let it lye, for as yet he shall sleepe ten dayes space.

Carry him out. 698b

Shift. How say you maister *Bryan*, shall I of him have the
gard?

698b *Cary him out.*] at l. 701 in Q

Bryan. By my troth Policie, thy good will to reward   700
In hope of thy just service, content I agree
For to resigne the keeping of this same Knight unto thee.
But give me thy hand that thou wilt deceive me never:
 Shift. Heres my hand, charme, inchant, make a spider catcher
of me, if I be false to you ever.   [*sig. D1*] 705
 Bryan. Well then come follow after me, and the gard of him
thou shalt have.

Exit.

 Shift. A thousand thanks I give you, this is all the promotion
I crave:
A sirrah, little knowes *Bryan,* that *Clamydes* my maister is,   710
But to set him free from prison I entend not to mis:
Yet still in my mind, I can do no other but muse,
What practise with my maisters apparell and shell he will use:
Well, seeing I have played the craftie knave with the one, ile play
it with the other: 715
Subtill *Shift* for advantage, will deceive his owne brother.

Exit.

[viii]

Here let them make a noyse as though they were
Marriners. And after Clyomon *Knight of G. S.*
come in with one.   720

 Clyomon [within]. Ah set me to shore sirs, in what countrey
so ever we bee.
 Shipmaister [within]. Well hayle out the Cockboate, seeing
so sicke we do him see,
Strike sayle, cast Ankers, till we have rigd our Ship againe,
For never were we in such stormes before, thats plaine.

Enter Clyomon, *Boateswaine.*   725

 Clyomon. Ah Boateswaine, gramercies for thy setting me
to shore

722 *Shipmaister.*] Dyce; *Shiftmai.* Q

Boateswaine. Truly Gentleman we were never in the like tempests before.

Clyomon. What countrey is this wherein now we be?

Boateswaine. Sure the Ile of strange Marshes, as our maister told to me.

Clyomon. How far is it from *Macedonia*, canst thou declare? 730

Boateswaine. More then twentie dayes sayling, and if the weather were faire.

Clyomon. Ah cruell hap of Fortunes spite, which signed this luck to me:

What Pallace Boateswaine is this same, canst thou declare, we see?

Boateswaine. There King *Patranius* keepes his Court, so farre as I do gesse,

And by this traine of Ladyes heere, I sure can judge no lesse. 735

Clyomon. Well Boateswaine, theres for thy paines, and here upon the shore

Ile lie to rest my wearie bones, of thee I crave no more.

Exit [*Boateswaine*].

Enter Neronis *daughter to* Patranius, *King of the*
strange Marshes, two Lords, two Ladies. 740

Neronis. My Lords, come will it please you walk abroad to take the pleasant ayre? [*sig. D1v*]

According to our wonted use, in fields both fresh and faire,

My Ladies here I know right well, will not gainsay the same.

1. Lord. Nor we sure for to pleasure you, *Neronis* noble Dame. 745

Neronis. Yes yes, men they love intreatie much, before they will be wonne.

2. Lord. No Princes that hath womens nature beene, since first the world begunne.

Neronis. So you say.

1. Lord. We boldly may, 750

738   *Exit.*] Dyce; at l. 736 in Q
747   nature] Dyce; natures Q

Under correction of your grace.

Neronis. Well, will it please you forth to trace,
That when we have of fragrant fields, the dulcet fumes obtained,
We may unto the Sea side go, whereas is to be gained,
More straunger sights among *Neptunes* waves, in seeing Ships
  to saile,   755
Which passe here by my fathers shore, with merrie westerne
  gaile.
1. Lord. We shall your highnesse leade the way to fields erst
  spoke before.
Neronis. Do so, and as we do returne weele come hard by the
  shore.

Exeunt.

Clyomon. What greater griefe can grow to gripe, the heart of
  greeved wight,   760
Then thus to see fell Fortune she, to hold his state in spight.
Ah cruell chance, ah lucklesse lot, to me poore wretch assign'd,
Was ever seene such contraries, by fraudulent Goddesse blind,
To any one save onely I, imparted for to be.
To amate the mind of any man, did ever Fortune she   765
Showe forth her selfe so cruell bent, as thus to keepe me backe,
From pointed place by weather driven, my sorrowes more to
  sacke.
Ah fatall hap, herein alas, what furder shall I say?
Since I am forced for to breake, mine oath and pointed day,
Before King *Alexanders* grace, *Clamydes* will be there,   770
And I through Fortunes cruell spight, opprest with sicknesse
  here:
For now within two dayes it is that we should meete togither,
Woe worth the wind and raging stormes, alas that brought me
  hither.
Now will *Clamides* me accuse, a faithlesse knight to be,
And eke report, that cowardlinesse did dant the heart of me.   775
The worthy praise that I have wonne, through fame shall be
  defaced,

765 amate] Dyce; animate Q

The name of the Knight of the Golden Sheeld, alas shall be dis-
graced,
Before that noble Prince of might, whereas *Clamydes* he
[*sig. D2*]
Will showe himselfe in Combat wise, for to exclaime on me,
For breaking of my poynted day, and *Clyomon* to thy greefe,
Now art thou in a countrey strange, cleane voyd of all releefe: 780
Opprest with sicknesse through the rage of stormie blasts and
cold,
Ah death come with thy direfull Mace, for longer to unfold
My sorrowes here it bootcth not, yet *Clyomon* do stay,
The Ladies loe, comes towards thee, that walkt the other way. 785

Enter Neronis, *two Lords, two Ladies.*

Neronis. Come faire dames, sith that we have in fragrant
fields obtained,
Of dulcet flowers the pleasant smell, and that these knights dis-
daincd
Not to beare us company, our walke more large to make,
Here by the sea of surging waves, our home returne weele make. 790
My Lords therefore do keepe your way.
1. Lord. As it please your grace we shall obey,
But behold Madame, what wofull sight, here in our way before,
As seemeth very sicke to me, doth lie upon the shore.
Neronis. My Lords, lets know the cause of greefe, whereof
he is oppressed: 795
That if he be a knight, it may by some meanes be redressed.
Faire sir well met, why lie you here? what is your cause of
griefe?
Clyomon. O Lady, sicknesse by the Sea, hath me opprest in
briefe.
Neronis. Of truth my Lords, his countenance bewrayes him
for to bee,
In health, of valiant heart and mind, and eke of hye degree. 800
2. Lord. It doth no lesse then so import, O Princes as you say.

777   disgraced] defaced Q

Neronis. Of whence are you? or whats your name? who
wander forth this way.

Clyomon. Of small valure O Lady faire, alas my name it is,
And for not telling of the same, hath brought me unto this.

Neronis. Why, for what cause sir Knight, shuld you not ex-   805
presse your name?

Clyomon. Because O Lady I have vowed, contrary to the
same.

But where I travell Lady faire, in Citie, Towne or field,
I am called, and do beare by name, the knight of the Golden
Shield.

Neronis. Are you that knight of the Golden sheeld, of whom
such fame doth go?   810

Clyomon. I am that selfesame knight faire dame, as here my
Sheeld doth show.

Neronis. Ah worthy then of helpe indeed, my Lords assist
I pray,

And to my lodging in the court, see that you him convey,

[*sig. D2v*]

For certainly within my minde, his state is much deplored,
But do dispaire in nought sir knight, for you shall be restored,   815
If Phisicke may your greefe redresse, for I *Neronis* loe,
Daughter to *Patranius* king, for that which fame doth shoe,
Upon your acts, will be your friend, as after you shall prove.

1. Lord. In doing so, you shall have meed of mightie Jove
above.

Clyomon. O Princes, if I ever be to health restord againe,   820
Your faithfull servant day and night, I vow here to remaine.

Neronis. Well my Lords, come after me, do bring him I require:

Ambo. We shall O Princes willingly accomplish your desire.

Exeunt.

[ix]

802   who] you Q
819   meed] Dyce; need Q

Enter Bryan sance foy, *having* Clamydes *his apparell*   825
on, his Sheeld, and the Serpents head.

Bryan. Ah sirrah, now is the ten dayes full expired, wherein
    Clamydes he,
Shall wake out of his charmed sleepe, as shortly you shall see:
But here I have what I desired, his Sheeld, his coat and head,
To *Denmarke* will I straight prepare, and there present with
    speed,   830
The same to *Julianas* grace, as in *Clamydes* name,
Whereby I am assur'd, I shall enjoy that noble Dame.
For why *Clamydes* he is safe, for ever being free,
And unto Knowledge is he left, here garded for to bee:
But no man knowes of my pretence, ne whither I am gone,   835
For secretly from Castle I, have stolne this night alone
In this order as you see, in the attire of a noble knight,
But yet poore *Bryan,* still thy heart holds courage in despight.
Well, yet the old proverbe to disprove, I purpose to begin,
Which alwayes sayth, that cowardly hearts, faire Ladies never
    win.   840
Shall I not *Juliana* win, and who hath a cowardlyer hart,
Yet for to brag and boast it out, ile will none take my part.
For I can looke both grim and fierce, as though I were of might,
And yet three Frogs out of a bush, my heart did so affright,
That I fell dead almost therewith, well, cowardly as I am,   845
Farewell Forrest, for now I will in knight *Clamydes* name,
To *Denmarke* to present this head, to *Juliana* bright,
Who shall a cowardly dastard wed, in steed of a worthy knight.

Exit.

[*sig. D3*]

[x]

Enter Shift *with sword and target.*   850

Shift. Be your leave I came up so early this morning that I
cannot see my way.
I am sure its scarce yet in the breake of the day.
But you muse I am sure wherefore these weapons I bring,

Well, listen unto my tale, and you shall know every thing.
Because I played the shifting knave, to save my selfe from
   harme,   855
And by my procurement, my maister was brought in this charme.
The ten dayes are exspir'd, and this morning he shall awake,
And now like a craftie knave, to the prison my way will I take,
With these same weapons, as though I would fight to set him
   free,   860
Which will give no occasion that he shall mistrust, there was
   deceit in mee.
And having the charge of him, here under *Bryan sance foy,*
Ile open the prison doores, and make as though I did imploy
To do it by force, through good will, and onely for his sake:
Then shall *Clamydes* being at liberty, the weapons of me take,   865
And set upon *Bryan* and all his men, now that they are a sleepe,
And so be revenged, for that he did him keepe
By charme in this order, so shall they both deceived be,
And yet upon neither part mistrust towards me.
Well, neere to the prison ile draw, to see if he be awake,   870
Harke, harke, this same is he, that his lamentation doth make.
   Clamydes in prison. Ah fatall hap, where am I wretch, in
     what distressed cace,
Bereft of Tyre, head and sheeld, not knowing in what place
My body is, ah heavenly gods, was ere such strangenes seene?
What do I dreame? or am I still within the forrest greene?   875
Dreame? no, no, alas I dreame not I, my senses all do faile,
The strangenes of this cruell hap, doth make my hart to quaile.
Clamydes ah by Fortune she, what froward luck and fate
Most cruelly assigned is, unto thy noble state.
Where should I be, or in what place hath desteny assignd   880
My sely corps for want of foode and comfort to be pind.
Ah farewell hope of purchasing my lady, since is lost,
The Serpents head whereby I should possesse that jewell most.

---

861   give no occasion ... there was deceit] give occasion ... there was no
     deceit Q
872   *Clamydes in prison.*] at ll. 872-3 in Q
873   Tyre] *Tyro* Q

Ah farewell hope of honour eke, now shall I breake my day
Before king *Alexanders* grace, whereon my faith doth stay. 885
[sig. D3v]
And shall I be found a faithlesse Knight, fye on fell Fortune she,
Which hath her wheele of froward chance, thus whirled back
on me.
Ah farewell King of *Swavia* land, ah farewell *Denmarke* dame,
Farewell thou Knight of the golden Sheeld, to thee shall rest
all fame.
To me this direfull desteny, to thee I know renowne, 890
To me the blast of ignomy, to thee Dame Honours crowne.
Ah hatefull hap, what shall I say, I see the gods hath signed
Through cruelty my carefull corps, in prison to be pined.
And nought alas amates me so, but that I know not where I am,
Nor how into this dolefull place my wofull body came. 895
    Shift. Alas good *Clamydes*, in what an admiration is he,
Not knowing in what place his body should be.
    Clamydes. Who nameth poore *Clamydes* there? reply to him
againe.
    Shift. Ant shall please you I am your servant Knowledge,
which in a thousand woes for you remaine. 900
    Clamydes. Ah Knowledge where am I declare and be briefe.
    Shift. Where are you? faith even in the Castle of that false
theefe
Bryan sance foy, against whome to fight and set you free,
Looke out at the windowe, behold I have brought tooles with
mee.
    Clamydes. Ah Knowledge, then cowardly that caitife did me
charme. 905
    Shift. Yea, or else he could never have done you any harme.
But be of good cheere, for such a shift I have made,
That the keyes of the prison I have got, your selfe perswade:
Wherewith this morning I am come to set you free,
And as they lye in their beds, you may murder *Bryan* and his
men, and set all other at libertie. 911
    Clamydes. Ah Knowledge, this hath me bound to be thy
friend for ever:

Shift. A true servant you may see will deceive his maister never.

So the doores are open, now come and follow after me.

Enter out. 914

Clamydes. Ah heavens, in what case my selfe do I see: 91

But speake Knowledge, canst thou tell how long have I bene heere?

Shift. These ten dayes full, and sleeping still, this sentence is most cleere.

Clamydes. Alas, then this same is the day the which appointed was

By the Knight of the golden Sheeld to me, that combat ours should passe

Before King *Alexanders* grace, and there I know he is: 92

Ah cruell Fortune why shouldst thou thus wrest my chance amis,

[*sig. D4*]

Knowing I do but honour seeke, and thou doest me defame,

In that contrary mine exspect, thou all things seekes to frame.

The faith and loyaltie of a knight thou causest me to breake,

Ah hatefull dame, why shouldst thou thus thy fury on me wreake.   92

Now will king *Alexander* judge the thing in me to bee,

The which since first I armes could beare, no wight did ever see.

But Knowledge give from thee to me, those weapons that I may

Upon that *Bryan* be reveng'd, which cowardly did betray

Me of my things, and heere from thrall all other knights set free   93

Whome he by charme did bring in bale, as erst he did by mee.

Come, into his lodging will I go, and challenge him and his.

Exit. 932

Shift. Do so, and to follow I will not mis.

Ah sirra, here was a shift according to my nature and condition,

And a thousand shifts more I have, to put my selfe out of sus-pition.   93

But it doth me good to thinke how that cowardly knave *Bryan sance foy*

Shall be taken in the snare, my hart doth even leape for joy.

Harke, harke, my maister is amongst them, but let him shift as
  he can,
For not to deale with a dog, he shall have help of his man.

Exit.

939b

Enter after a little fight within, Clamydes, three
knights.

(sd) 940

Clamydes. Come, come sir Knights, for so unfortunate was
  never none as I,
That I should joy that is my joy, the heavens themselves deny.
That cowardly wretch that kept you here, and did me so deceive,
Is fled away and hath the Sheeld, the which my Lady gave
To me in token of her love, the Serpents head like case   945
For which this mine adventure was, to winne her noble grace.
  1. Knight. And sure that same th'occasion was, why we
  adventred hether.
  Clamydes. Well, sith I have you delivered, when as you please
  together
Each one into his native soile his journey do prepare,
For though that I have broke my day as erst I did declare,   950
Through this most cowardly catifes charmes, in meeting of the
  Knight,
Which of the golden Sheeld beares name, to know else what he
  hight:
I will to *Alexanders* court, and if that thence he be,
Yet will I seeke to finde him out, least he impute to me
Some cause of cowardlinesse to be, and therefore sir Knights
  depart: 955
As to my selfe I wish to you with fervent zeale of hart,
Yet if that any one of you do meete this Knight by way [*sig. D4v*]
What was the cause of this my let, let him perstand I pray.
  Omnes. We shall not misse O noble Knight, to accomplish
  this your will.

Exeunt.

960

Clamydes. Well then adue sir Knights each one, the gods
protect you still.
What Knowledge ho, where art thou man? come forth that hence
we may.
Shift within. Where am I? faith breaking open of chests here
within, for ile have the spoile of all away.
Clamydes. Tush, tush, I pray thee come that hence we may,   96!
no riches thou shalt lacke.

[*Enter*] Shift *with a bag as it were full of gold on his backe.*   966t

[*Shift.*] I come now with as much money as I am able to carry
of my backe.
A there was never poore asse so loden, but how now, that
cowardly *Bryan* have you slaine?   97(
And your Sheeld, the Serpents head, and coate, have you againe?
Clamydes. Ah no Knowledge, the knights that here were
captives kept, they are by me at libertie,
But that false *Bryan* this same night, is fled away for certaintie,
And hath all things he tooke from me, convayed where none doth
know.   97!
Shift. O the bones of me, how will you then do for the Ser-
pents head to *Juliana* to show?
Clamydes. I have no other hope alas, but onely that her grace
Will credit give unto my words, when as I shew my cace
How they were lost, but first ere I unto that dame returne,   98(
Ile seeke the knight of the golden Sheeld, whereas he doth so-
journe,
To accomplish what my father wild, and therefore come away.

                              Exit.   982t

Shift. Well, keepe on before, for I mind not to stay.
A sirra, the craftier knave, the better lucke, thats plaine.
I have such a deale of substance here, where *Bryans* men are
slaine,   985

966b   Shift ... *backe*] at ll. 967-969 in Q

That it passeth. O that I had while for to stay,
I could lode a hundreth carts full of kitchingstuffe away.
Well, its not best to tary too long behinde, lest my maister over-go,
And then some knave knowing of my money, a peece of cosonage
    sho.

Exit.   990

[xi]

Enter Neronis.

Neronis. How can that tree but withered be
       That wanteth sap to moist the roote?   [*sig. E1*]
   How can that Vine but waste and pine
       Whose plants are troden under foote?   995
   How can that spray but soone decay,
       That is with wild weeds overgrowne?
   How can that wight in ought delight
       Which showes, and hath no good will showne?

   Or else how can that heart alasse,   1000
       But die by whom each joy doth passe?

Neronis, ah I am the Tree, which wanteth sap to moyst the
    roote.
Neronis, ah I am the vine, whose Plants are troden under foote.
I am the spray which doth decay, and is with wild weeds over-
    growne,
I am the wight without delight, which shows, and hath no good
    wil showne.   1005
Mine is the heart by whom alas, each pleasant joy doth passe,
Mine is the heart which vades away, as doth the flower or grasse.
In wanting sap to moyst the roote, is joyes that made me glad,
And plants being troden under foote, is pleasures that was had.
I am the spray which doth decay, whom cares have overgrowne, 1010
But stay *Neronis,* thou saist thou showest, and hath no good will
    showne:

Why so I do, how can I tell, *Neronis* force no crueltie
Thou seest thy knight endued is, with all good gifts of courtesie:
And doth *Neronis* love indeed, to whom love doth she yeeld,
Even to that noble brute of fame, the knight of the golden Sheeld. 1015
Ah wofull Dame, thou knowest not thou, of what degree he is,
Of noble bloud his gesters showe, I am assured of this.
Why belike he is some runnagate that will not show his name,
Ah why should I this allegate, he is of noble fame.
Why dost thou not expresse thy love, to him *Neronis* then? 1020
Because shamefastnesse and womanhood, bids us not seek to
    men.
Ah carefull Dame loe thus I stand, as twere one in a trance,
And lacketh boldnesse for to speake, which should my words
    advance.
The knight of the Golden Sheeld it is, to whom a thrall I am,
Whom I to health restored have, since that to court he cam. 1025
And now he is prest to passe againe, upon his wearie way,
Unto the Court of *Alexander*, yet hath he broke his day,
As he to me the whole exprest, ah sight that doth me greeve,
Loe where he comes to passe away, of me to take his leave.

[*sig. E1v*]

Enter Clyomon. 1030

Clyomon. Who hath more cause to praise the Gods, then I
whose state deplored?
Through phisicke and *Neronis* helpe, to health am now restored:
Whose servent thrall I am become, yet urgent causes dooth
Constraine me for to keepe it close, and not to put in proofe 1035
What I might do to winne her love, as first my oath and vow,
In keeping of my name unknowne, which she will not allow:
If I should seeme to breake my minde, being a Princes borne,
To yeeld her love to one unknowne, I know sheele thinke it
    scorne:
Besides here longer in this Court, alas I may not stay, 1040
Although that with *Clamydes* he, I have not kept my day:
Least this he should suppose in me, for cowardlinesse of hart,
To seeke him out elsewhere, I will from out this Land depart.

Yet though unto *Neronis* she, I may not shew my mind,
A faithfull heart when I am gone, with her I leave behind.   1045
Whose bountiousnesse I here have felt, but since I may not stay,
I will to take my leave of her, before I passe away.
Loe where she walkes, O Princesse well met, why are you here
    so sad?
Neronis. Good cause I have, since pleasures passe, the which
    shuld make me glad.
Clyomon. What you should meane, O Princesse deare, hereby
    I do not know.   1050
Neronis. Then listen to my talke a while, Sir Knight and I
    will show.
If case you will reaunswere me, my question to absolve,
The which propound within my mind, doth oftentimes revolve.
Clyomon. I will O Princes answere you as aptly as I may.
Neronis. Well then Sir Knight, apply your eares, and listen
    what I say: 1055
A ship that stormes had tossed long, amidst the mounting waves,
Where harbour none was to be had, fell Fortune so depraves,
Through ill successe that ship of hope, that Ancors hold doth
    faile,
Yet at the last shees driven to land, with broken Mast and saile:
And through the force of furious wind, and Billowes bounsing
    blowes,   1060
She is a simple shipwracke made, in every point God knowes.
Now this same ship by chance being found, the finders take such
    paine,
That fit to saile upon the Seas, they rig her up againe.
And where she was through storms fore shakt, they make her
    whole and sound:
Now answere me directly here, upon this my propound.   1065
                                                    [*sig. E2*]
If this same ship thus rent and torne, being brought in former
    rate,
Should not supply the finders turn to profit his estate

1052 absolve] obsolve Q
1067 turn] Dyce; true Q

In what she might — — —
   Clyomon. Herein a right,
I will O Princesse as I may, directly answere you.   1070
This ship thus found, I put the case it hath an owner new,
Which owner shall sufficiently content the finders charge:
And have againe to serve his use, his ship, his boate or barge.
The ship then cannot serve the turne of finders, this is plaine,
If case the owner do content, or pay him for his paine.   1075
But otherwise if none lay claime, nor seeme that ship to stay,
Then is it requisit it should, the finders paines repay:
For such endevour as it is to serve for his behoofe.
   Neronis. What owner truly that it hath, I have no certaine
proofe.
   Clyomon. Then can I not define thereof, but thus I wish it
were,   1080
That you would me accept to be, that ship O Lady faire:
And you the finder, then it should be needlesse for to moove,
If I the ship, of dutie ought to serve at your behoove.
   Neronis. Thou art the ship O worthy Knight, so shivered
found by mee.
   Clyomon. And owner have I none deare dame, I yeeld me
whole to thee: 1085
For as this ship I must confesse, that was a shipwrack made,
Thou hast restored me unto health, whom sicknesse causd to
vade,
For which I yeeld O Princesse deare, at pleasure thine to be,
If your grace, O noble Dame, will so accept of me.
   Neronis. If case I will what have you showne?   1090
   Clyomon. Because I am to you unknowne.
   Neronis. Your fame importeth what you be.
   Clyomon. You may your pleasure say of me.
   Neronis. What I have said due proofs do showe.
   Clyomon. Well Lady deare, to thee I owe   1095
More service then of dutie I am able to professe,
For that thou didst preserve my life amidst my deepe distresse:

1071   new] now Q
1094   proofs] Bullen; proofe Q

But at this time I may not stay. O Lady here with thee,
Thou knowest the cause, but this I vow within three score dayes
   to bee,
If destinie restraine me not, at court with thee againe,   1100
Protesting whilest that life doth last, thine faithfull to remaine.
                                    [*sig. E2v*]
   Neronis. And is there then no remedie, but needs you will
   depart?
   Clyomon. No Princesse for a certaintie, but here I leave my
   hart,
In gage with thee till my returne, which as I said shall be:
   Neronis. Well, sith no perswasion may prevaile, this Jewell
   take of me,   1105
And keepe it always for my sake.
   Clyomon. Of it a deare account ile make, yet let us part deare
   Dame with joy,
And to do the same I will my selfe imploy.
   Neronis. Well now adieu till thy returne, the Gods thy journey
   guide,
                     Exit.   1109b

   Clyomon. And happily in absence mine, for thee deare Dame
   provide: 1110
Ah *Clyomon* let dolours die, drive daunts from out thy mind,
Since in the sight of Fortune now, such favour thou dost find,
As for to have the love of her whom thou didst sooner judge,
Would have denied thy loyaltie, and gainst thy good will grudge,
But that I may here keepe my day, you sacred Gods provide, 1115
Most happie fate unto my state, and thus my journey guide:
The which I tempt to take in hand *Clamydes* for to meete:
That the whole cause of my first let, to him I may repeate.
So shall I seeme for to excuse my selfe in way of right,
And not be counted of my foe, a false perjured Knight.
                     Exit.   1120b

[xii]

Enter Thrasellus *King of Norway, two Lords.* 1121

Thrasellus. Where deepe desire hath taken roote, my Lords
alas you see,
How that perswasion booteth not, if contrarie it be
Unto the first expected hope, where fancie hath take place,
And vaine it is for to withdraw, by counsell in that case, 112?
The mind who with affection is, to one onely thing affected,
The which may not till dint of death, from there be sure rejected:
You know my lords through fame, what force of love hath taken
place,
Within my breast as touching now *Neronis* noble grace,
Daughter to *Patranius* King, who doth the Scepter sway, 113(
And in the Ile of Marshes eke, beare rule now at this day.
Through love of daughter his, my sorrowes daily grow,
And daily dolours do me daunt, for that alas I show
Such Friendship whereas favour none, is to be found againe:
And yet from out my carefull mind, nought may her love re-
straine. 1135
I sent to crave her of the king, he answered me with nay:
But shall I not provide by force to fetch her thence away?
[*sig. E3*]
Yes, yes, my Lords, and therefore let your aydes be prest with
mine,
For I will sure *Neronis* have, or else my dayes ile pine.
For King *Patranius* and his power, I hold of small account, 1140
To winne his daughter to my spouse, amids his men ile mount.
1. Lord. Most worthy Prince, this rash attempt, I hold not
for the best,
For sure *Patranius* power is great, and not to be supprest.
For why, the ile environd is, with sea on every side,
And landing place lo is there none, whereas you may have tide 1145
To set your men from ship to shore, but by one onely way,
And in that place a garison great, he keepeth at this day.
So that if you should bring your power, your travell were in vaine,

1127 there] them Q

That is not certainly the way, *Neronis* for to gaine.
But this your grace may do indeed, and so I count it best, 1150
To be in all points with a Ship, most like a Merchant prest:
And saile with such as you thinke best, all drest in Merchants
guise,
And for to get her to your Ship, some secret meane devise,
By shewing of strange Merchandies, or other such like thing,
Lo this is best advise I can, *Thrassellus* Lord and King. 1155
   2. Lord. And certainly as you have sayd, my Lord it is the
way,
Wherefore O King, do prosecute the same without delay.
   Thrasellus. Of truth my Lords this your advise doth for our
purpose frame,
Come therefore let us hence depart, to put in ure the same
With present speed, for Merchant-wise my selfe will thither saile: 1160
   1. Lord. This is the way if any be, of purpose to prevaile.

Exeunt.

[xiii]

Enter Clyomon *with a Knight, signifying one of those
that* Clamydes *had delivered.*

   Clyomon. Sir Knight, of truth this fortune was most luckely
assignd, 1165
That we should meete in travell thus, for thereby to my mind
You have a castle of comfort brought, in that you have me told,
Clamydes our appointed day, no more then I did hold.
   Knight. No certis sir he kept not day, the cause I have ex-
pressed,
Through that inchanter *Bryans* charmes, he came full sore
distressed: 1170
Yet fortune favored so his state, that through his help all wee
Which captives were through cowardly craft, from bondage were
set free:
And at our parting willed us, if any with you met, [*sig. E3v*]
We should informe you with the truth what was his onely let.

Clyomon. Well, know you where he abideth now, sir Knight
I crave of curtesie?   117ʃ
Knight. No questionlesse I know not I, to say it of a certaintie.
Clyomon. Well then adue sir Knight with thanks, I let you
on your way:
Knight: Unto the gods I you commit, nought else I have to
say.

Exit.

Clyomon. A sirra, now the hugie heapes of cares that lodged
in my mind   118(
Is skaled from their nestling place, and pleasures passage find.
For that as well as *Clyomon, Clamydes* broke his day,
Upon which newes my passage now in seeking him ile stay:
And to *Neronis* back againe, my joyfull journey make,
Least that she should in absence mine, some cause of sorrow take. 118ʃ
And now all dumps of deadly dole, that danted knightly brest,
Adue, since salve of solace sweete, hath sorrowes all supprest,
For that *Clamydes* cannot brag, nor me accuse in ought:
Unto the gods of destenies, that thus our fates hath brought
In equall ballance to be wayed, due praises shall I send   119(
That thus to way each cause aright, their eyes to earth did bend.
Well, to keepe my day with Lady now, I mind not to be slack,
Wherefore unto *Patranius* court, ile dresse my journey back.
But stay, me thinks I *Rumor* heare throughout this land to ring,
I will attend his talke, to know what tidings he doth bring.

Enter Rumor *running.*   119(

[*Rumor.*] Ye rowling Clowdes give *Rumor* roome, both ayre
and earth below,
Both sea and land, that every eare may understand and know,
What wofull hap is chaunced now within the ile of late,
Which of strange Marshes beareth name, unto the noblest state. 120(
Neronis daughter to the King, by the King of *Norway* he,
Within a ship of Marchandise, convayed away is she.
The King with sorow for her sake, hath to death resignd,

1197   Both] By Q

And having left his Queene with child, to guide the realm behind,
Mustantius brother to the King, from her the Crowne would take,   1205
But till she be delivered, the Lords did order make,
That they before King *Alexander*, thither comming should ap-
    peale,
And he by whom they hold the crowne, therein should rightly
    deale
For either part, lo this to tell, I *Rumor* have in charge,   [*sig. E4*]
And through all lands I do pretend, to publish it at large.   1210

                    Exit.   1210b

Clyomon. Ah wofull *Rumor* raunging thus, what tidings do
    I heare,
Hath that false King of *Norway* stolne my love and Lady deare?
Ah hart, ah hand, ah head and mind, and every sence beside,
To serve your maisters turne in need, do every one provide:
For till that I revenged be upon that wretched king,   1215
And have againe my Lady deare, and her from *Norway* bring,
I vow this body takes no rest, ah Fortune fickle dame,
That canst make glad and so soone sad, a Knight of worthie fame.
But what should I delay the time, now that my deare is gone?
Availeth ought to ease my griefe, to make this pensive mone?   1220
No, no, wherefore come courage to my heart, and happie hands
    prepare,
For of that wretched King I will wreake all my sorow and care.
And mauger all the might he may, be able for to make,
By force of armes my lady I, from him and his will take.

                    Exit.   1224b

                    [xiv]

    Enter Clamydes *and* Shift, *with his bag of money still.*   1225

Clamydes. Come Knowledge, thou art much to blame, thus
    for to lode thy selfe
To make thee on thy way diseased, with carying of that pelfe.

But now take courage unto thee, for to that ile I will,
Which of strange Marshes called is, for fame declareth still
The Knight of the golden Sheeld is there, and in the court abideth, 1230
Thither will I him to meete, whatsoever me betideth:
And know his name, as thou canst tell my father charged me,
Or else no more his princely court nor person for to see.
Come therefore, that unto that ile we may our journey take,
And afterwards having met with him, our viage for to make   1235
To *Denmarke* to my Lady there, to shew her all my cace,
And then to *Swavia* if her I have, unto my fathers grace.

    Shift. Nay but ant shall please you, are you sure the Knight
of the golden Sheeld in the ile of Strange Marshes is?

    Clamydes. I was informed credibly, I warrant thee we shall
not mis.   1240

Exit.

    Shift. Then keepe on your way, ile follow as fast as I can,
Faith he even meanes to make a martris of poore *Shift* his man.
And I am so tied to this bag of gold I got at *Bryan sance foyes,*
That I tell you where this is, there all my joy is: [*sig.* E4v] 1245
But I am so weary, sometimes with ryding, sometimes with run-
ning, and other times going a foote,
That when I come to my lodging at night, to bring me a woman
it is no boote.
And such care I take for this pelfe, least I should it lose,
That where I come, that it is gold, for my life I dare not disclose. 1250
Well after my maister I must, heeres nothing stil but running
and ryding:
But ile give him the slip sure, if I once come where I may have
quiet biding.

Exit.

[xv]

    Enter Neronis *in the Forrest, in mans apparell.*   1254

    Neronis. As Hare the Hound, as Lambe the Wolfe, as foule
the Fawcons dint,

So do I flie from tyrant he, whose heart more hard then flint
Hath sackt on me such hugie heapes of seaceles sorrowes here,
That sure it is intollerable, the torments that I beare:
Neronis, ah who knoweth thee, a Princes to be borne,
Since fatall Gods so frowardly, thy fortune doth adorne: 1260
Neronis, ah who knoweth her, in painfull Pages show?
But no good Lady wil me blame, which of my case doth know:
But rather when they heare the truth, wherefore I am disguised,
Thaile say it is an honest shift, the which I have devised:
Since I have given my faith and troth to such a brute of fame,   1265
As is the knight of the Golden Shield, and tyrants seekes to frame
Their engins to detract our vowes, as the king of Norway hath,
Who of all Princes living now, I finde devoyd of faith:
For like a wolfe in lambes skin clad, he commeth with his aide,
All Marchant like to fathers Court, and ginneth to perswade   1270
That he had precious jewels brought which in his ship did lye,
Whereof he wild me take my choyce, if case I would them buy:
Then I mistrusting no deceit, with handmaids one or two
With this deceitfull Marchant then unto the ship did go.
No sooner were we under hatch, but up they hoyst their saile, 1275
And having then to serve their turne, a mery Westerne gaile:
We were lasht out from the haven, lo a dosen leagues and more,
When still I thought the Barke had bene, at anker by the shore:
But being brought by Norway here, not long in Court I was
But that to get from thence away, I brought this feate to passe: 1280
For making semblance unto him as though I did him love,
He gave me libertie, or ought that serv'd for my behove: [sig. F1]
And having libertie, I wrought by such a secret flight,
That in this tyre like to a page, I scapt away by night.
But ah I feare that by pursute, he wil me overtake,   1285
Well here entreth one, to whom some sute for service I wil make.

Enter Corin *a Shepheard.*

Corin. Gos bones turne in that sheep there and you be good
  fellowes, Jesu how cham beraide,
Chave a cur here, an a were my vellow, cha must him conswade, 1290

1271   brought] Dyce; bought Q

And yet an cha should kisse, looke you of the arse, cha must run
my selfe an chil,
An cha should entreat him with my cap in my hand ha wad stand
stil.
But tis as world to zee what mery lives we shepheards lead,
Why were Gentlemen and we get once a thorne bush over our
head,
We may sleep with our vaces against the zone, and were hogs 1295
Bath our selves, stretch out our legs ant were a cennell of dogs:
And then at night when maides come to milkin, the games begin,
But I may zay to you, my nabor *Hodges* maid had a clap, wel let
them laugh that win.
Chave but one daughter, but chould not vor vorty pence she were
zo sped,
Cha may zay to you, she lookes every night to go to bed: 1300
But tis no matter, the whores be so whiskish when thare under a
bush,
That thare never satisfied, til their bellies be flush.
Well cha must abroad about my flocks, least the fengeance wolves
catch a lambe:
Vor by my cursen zoule, thale steale an cha stand by, there not
averd of the dam.
  Neronis. Wel to scape the pursute of the king, of this same
shepheard here,   1305
Suspition wholly to avoyd, for service ile enquire:
Wel met good father, for your use, a servant do you lacke?
  Corin. What you wil not flout an old man you courtnold Jacke?
  Neronis. No truly father I flout you not, what I aske I would
have.
  Corin. Gos bones they leest, serve a shepheard an be zo brave? 1310
You courtnoll crackropes, wod be hangd, you do nothing now
and then
But come up and downe the country, thus to flout poore men.
Go too goodman boy, chave no zervis vor no zuch flouting Jacks
as you be.

1294   were] where Q
1298   *Hodges*] Dyce; *Hogs* Q

Neronis. Father I thinke as I speake, upon my faith and troth
beleeve me,
I wil willingly serve you, if in case you wil take me.　　　　1315
Corin. Doest not mocke?
Neronis. No truly father.
Corin. Then come with me, by gosbones chil never vorsake
thee.　　　　　　　　　　　　　　　　　　　　　[*sig. F1v*]
Whow bones of my zoule, thowilt be the bravest shepherds boy in
our town,
Thous go to church in this coate, bevore *Madge* a sonday in her
gray gown.　　　　1320
God lord how our church-wardens wil looke upon thee, bones of
god zeest,
There will be more looking at thee, then our sir John the parish
preest.
Why everybody wil aske whose boy thart, an cha can tel the this
by the way,
Thou shalt have al the varest wenches of our town in the veelds
vor to play.
Theres nabour *Nychols* daughter, a jolly smug whore with vat
cheekes,　　　　1325
And nabour *Hodges* maide, meddle not with her, she hath eaten
set leekes.
But theres *Frumptons* wench in the freese sacke, it will do thee
good to see
What canvosing is at the milking time, betweene her and mee.
And those wenches will love thee bonnomablely in every place,
But do not vall in with them in any kind of cace.　　　　1330
　　Neronis. Tush, you shall not neede to feare me, I can be mery
with measure as well as they:
　　Corin. Wel then come follow after me, and home chil leade
thee the way.
　　Neronis. Alas poore simple Shepheard, by this Princes may
see,
That like man, like talke, in every degree.　　　　1335

Exeunt.

[xvi]

Enter Thrasellus *King of Norway, and two Lords.*

Thrasellus. My Lords pursue her speedely, she cannot far
be gone,
And lo himselfe to seeke her out, your King he will be one.
Ah fraudulent dame, how hath she glozd, from me to get away?
With sugred words how hath she fed, my senses night and day? 1340
Professing love with outward showes, and inwardly her hart
To practise such a deepe deceit, whereby she might depart
From out my court so sodainly, when I did wholy judge
She loved me most entirely, and not against me grudge.
She made such signes by outward showes, I blame not wit and
policie,   1345
But here I may exclame and say, fye, fye in womens subtiltie.
Well well my Lords no time delay, pursue her with all speed,
And I this forest will seeke out my selfe, as is decreed,
With aide of such as are behind, and will come unto mee: 1349
    Ambo. We shal not slake what here in charge to us is given
by thee.

                    Exeunt.   1350b

Thrasellus. Ah subtill *Neronis,* how hast thou me vexed?
Through thy crafty dealings how am I perplexed?
Did ever any winne a dame, and lose her in such sort?
The maladies are marvellous, the which I do support   [*sig. F2*]
Through her deceit, but forth I will my company to meete,   1355
If ever she be caught againe, I will her so intreate,
That others all shall warning take, by such a subtill dame,
How that a Prince for to delude, such ingins they do frame.

      Enter Clyomon *Knight of the golden Sheeld.*

Clyomon. Nay Traytour stay, and take with thee that mortall
blow or stroke: 1360
The which shall cause thy wretched corps this life for to revoke.
It joyeth me at the hart that I have met thee in this place.

Thrasellus. What varlet darest thou be so bold, with words in
such a cace,
For to upbraide thy Lord and King? what art thou soone declare?
Clyomon. My Lord and King, I thee defie, and in despite I
dare   1365
Thee for to say thou art no Prince, for thou a Traytour art,
And what reward is due therefore, to thee I shall impart.
Thrasellus. Thou braggest all too boldly still, what hight thy
name expresse?
Clyomon. What hight my name thou shalt not know, ne will
I it confesse:
But for that thou my Lady stolest from fathers court away,   1370
Ile sure revenge that trayterous fact upon thy flesh this day.
Since I have met so luckely with thee here all alone,
Although as I do understand, from thee she now is gone,
Yet therefore do defend thy selfe, for here I thee assaile.
Thrasellus. Alas poore boy, thinkest thou against me to pre-
vaile?   1375

Here let them fight, the King fall downe dead.

Thrasellus. Ah heavens, *Thrasellus* he is slaine, ye Gods his
ghost receive.
Clyomon. Now hast thou justice for thy fact, as thy desert
doeth crave:
But ah alas poore *Clyomon*, though thou thy foe hast slaine,
Such greevous wounds thou hast receiv'd, as doth increase thy
paine.   1380
Unles I have some speedy help, my life must needly wast,
And then as well as traytour false, my corps of death shall tast.
Ah my *Neronis* where art thou? ah where art thou become?
For thy sweete sake thy Knight shall here receive his vitall doome.
Lo here all gorde in bloud thy faithfull Knight doth lye,   1385
For thee, ah faithfull dame, thy Knight for lack of help shall dye.
For thee, ah here thy *Clyomon*, his mortall stroke hath tane,
For thee, ah these same hands of his, the *Norway* King hath slaine.
Ah bleeding wounds from longer talke my foltring tong doth stay,
And if I have not speedy help, my life doth wast away.   [*sig. F2v*] 1390

Enter father Corin *the Shepheard, and his dog.*

Corin.   A plage on thee for a cur, a ha driven me sheepe above
from the flocke:
A theefe, art not asham'd? ile beate thee like a stocke:
And cha beene azeeking here, above voure miles and more:
But chill tell you what, chave the bravest lad of Jack the court-
   noll, that ever was zeene bevore.   1395
A, the whorcop is plagely well lov'd in our towne,
An you had zeene go to Church bevore *Madge* my wife in her
   holyday gowne,
You would have blest your zelves t'ave seene it, he went even
   cheke by joule
With our head controms wife, brother to my nabour *Nycholl,*   1400
You know ha dwels by maister Justice, over the water on the other
side of the hill,
Cham zure you know it, betweene my nabour *Filchers* varme
house, and the wind-mill.
But an you did zee how *Jone Jenkin,* and *Gilian Giffrey* loves
   my boy Jacke,   1405
Why it is marvelation to see, *Jone* did so bast *Gillians* backe,
That by Gos bones I laught till cha be pist my zelfe, when cha
   zaw it:
All the maides in towne valls out for my boy, but and the yongmen
   know it,
Thale be zo jelisom over them, that cham in doubt
Ich shall not keepe Jack my boy till seven yeares go about.   1410
Well, cham nere the neere vor my shepe, chave sought it this voure
   mile,
But chill home, and send Jack foorth to zeeke it another while.
But bones of God man stay, Jesu whither wilt? wha what meanst
   lye heere?
Clyomon.   Ah good father help me.
Corin.   Nay who there, by your leave, chill not come neere.   1415
What another? bones of me, he is either kild or dead?

1399   he] she Q
1413   whither] whather Q

Nay varewell vorty pence, yeare a knave, gos death a doth bleede.

Clyomon. I bleede indeede father, so grievous my wounds bee,
That if I have not speedie help, long life is not in mee.

  Corin. Why what art thou? or how chanst thou camst in this
  cace?   1420

  Clyomon. Ah father, that dead corps which thou seest there
  in place,

He was a Knight, and mine enemy, whom here I have slaine,
And I a Gentleman, whom he hath wounded with marvellous
  paine.
Now thou knowest the truth, good father shew some curtesie
To stop my bleeding wounds, that I may finde some remedie, 1425
My life to preserve, if possible I may: [*sig. F3*]

  Corin. Well heare you gentleman, chould have you know this
  by the way,

Cham but vather *Coryn* the sheepheard, cham no surringer I,
But chill do what cha can vor you, cha were loth to see you die.
Loe how zay you by this, have cha done you any ease? 1430

  Clyomon. Father thy willingnesse of a certaintie, doth me
  much please:

But good father lend me thy helping hand once againe,
To burie this same Knight whom here I have slaine,
Although he was to me a most deadly enemie,
Yet to leave his body unburied, were great crueltie.   1435

  Corin. Bones of God man, our Priest dwells too farre away.

  Clyomon. Well, then for want of a Priest, the Priests part I
  will play:

Therefore father helpe me to lay his body aright,
For I will bestow a herse of him, because he was a Knight:
If thou wilt go to a Cottage hereby, and fetch such things as I
  lacke.   1440

  Corin. That chill Gentleman, and by and by returne backe.

Exit.

  Clyomon. But *Clyomon* pluck up thy heart, with courage once
  againe,

And I will set over his dead Coarse in signe of victorie,

My Golden Sheeld and Sword, but with the poynt hanging downe, 1445
As one conquered and lost his renowne.
Writing likewise thereupon, that all passengers may see,
That the false King of *Norway*, here lieth slaine by me.

Enter Corin *with a Hearse.*

Corin. Lo Gentleman, cha brought zuch things, as are requisit
for the zame: 1450
Clyomon. Then good father helpe me, the Hearse for to frame.
Corin. That chall Gentleman, in the best order that cha may:
O that our Parish Preest were here, that you might heare him say,
Vor by gos bones, an there be any noyse in the Church, in the
midst of his prayers heele sweare.   1455
A he loves hunting a life, would to God you were acquainted
with him a while,
And as vor a woman, well chill zay nothing, but cha knowe whom
hee did beguile.
Clyomon. Well father *Coryn* let that passe, wee have nothing
to do withall,   1460
And now that this is done, come reward thy paine I shall.
There is part of a recompence, thy good will to requite. [*sig. F3v*]
Corin. By my troth cha thank you, cham bound to pray vor
you day and night.
And now chil even home, and send Jack my boy this sheep to
seek out:
Clyomon. Tell me father ere thou goest, didst thou not see a
Lady wandring here about?   1465
Corin. A Lady no good vaith gentleman, cha zaw none cha
tel you plane:

[*Exit* Corin.]

Clyomon. Wel then farewell father, gramercies for thy paine.
Ah *Neronis* where thou art, or where thou doest abide,
Thy *Clyomon* to seeke thee out, shall rest no time nor tide: 1470

1452   *Corin.*] Dyce; omitted in Q
1452   That] Chat Q

Thy foe here lieth slaine on ground, and living is thy frend,
Whose travel til he see thy face, shall never have an end.
My Ensigne here I leave behind, these verses writ shall yeeld
A true report of traytor slaine, by the knight of the golden sheeld.
And as unknowne to any wight, to travell I betake,   1475
Until I may her find, whose sight my hart may joyfull make.

Exit.   1476b

[xvii]

Enter Shift *very brave.*

Shift. Jesu what a gazing do you make at me, to see me in a
gowne?
Do you not know after travell, men being in Court or in Towne,
And specially such as is of any reputation, they must use this guise, 1480
Which signifieth a foole to be sage, grave, and of counsell wise.
But where are we thinke you now, that *Shift* is so brave?
Not running to seeke the knight of the golden sheeld, an other
office I have:
For comming here to the court, of strange Marshes so named,
Where King *Alexander* in his owne person lies, that Prince mightily
famed,   1485
Between *Mustantius* brother to the late king deceased
And the Queene, through King *Alexander*, a strife was appeased:
But how or which way I thinke you do not know,
Well then give eare to my tale, and the truth I wil show:
The old King being dead, through sorrow for *Neronis*,   1490
Whom we do heare, Lover to the Knight of the Golden Sheeld is,
The Queene being with child, the scepter asked to sway,
But *Mustantius* the Kings brother, he did it denay.
Whereof great contention grew, amongst the Nobles on either
side,
But being by them agreed the judgement to abide   1495
Of King *Alexander* the great, who then was comming hither,
At his arrivall to the Court, they all were cald togither.
The matter being heard, this sentence was given,   [*sig. F4*]

That either partie should have a Champion to combat them be-
tweene:
That which Champion were overcome, the other should sway,   1500
And to be foughten after that time, the sixteene day.
Now my maister *Clamydes* comming hither, for *Mustantius* wil
he bee,
But upon the Queenes side, to venter none can we see:
And yet she maketh proclamation through every land,
To give great gifts to any that will take the combat in hand.   1505
Well within ten daies is the time, and king *Alexander* hee
Staieth till the day appointed, the triall to see:
And if none come at the day for the Queene to fight,
Then without travel to my maister, *Mustantius* hath his right.
But to see all things in a readines, against thappointed day: 1510
Like a shifting knave for advantage, to Court Ile take my way.

Exit.

[xviii]

Enter Neronis *like a Sheepheards boy.*

Neronis.   The painfull pathes, the wearie wayes, the travels and
ill fare,
That simple seeme, to Princes feete in practise verie rare,   1515
As I poore Dame, whose pensive heart, no pleasure can delight,
Since that my state so cruelly, fell Fortune holds in spight.
Ah poore *Neronis* in thy hand, is this a seemely showe,
Who shouldst in Court thy Lute supplie, where pleasures erst
did flowe?
Is this an instrument for thee to guide a sheepheards flocke?   1520
That art a Princes by thy birth, and borne of noble stocke.
May mind from mourning more refraine, to thinke on former
state?
May heart from sighing eke abstaine, to see this simple rate?
May eyes from downe distilling teares, when thus a lone I am,

1508   come] came Q
1515   simple seeme, to Princes feete] simple feete, to Princes seeme Q
1524   a lone] Dyce; a loue Q

Resistance make, but must they not, through ceaselesse sorrowes
    frame   1525
A River of distilled drops, for to bedew my face?
A heavens when you are revengd inough, then looke upon my
    cace:
For till I heare some newes alas upon my loving Knight,
I dare not leave this loathsome life, for feare of greater spight:
And now as did my maister will, a sheepe that is a stray   1530
I must go seeke her out againe, by wild and wearie way. [*sig. F4v*]
Ah wofull sight, what is alas, with these mine eyes beheld,
That to my loving Knight belongd, I view the Golden Sheeld:
Ah heavens, this Herse doth signifie my Knight is slaine,
Ah death no longer do delay, but rid the lives of twaine: 1535
Heart, hand, and everie sence prepare, unto the Hearse draw nie:
And thereupon submit your selves, disdaine not for to die
With him that was your mistresse joy, her life and death like case,
And well I know in seeking me, he did his end embrace.
That cruell wretch that *Norway* King, this cursed deed hath
    dunne,   1540
But now to cut that lingring threed, that *Lachis* long hath spunne,
The sword of this my loving knight, behold I here do take,
Of this my wofull corps alas, a finall end to make:
Yet ere I strike that deadly stroke, that shall my life deprave,
Ye muses ayd me to the Gods, for mercie first to crave.   1545

Sing heere.

Well now you heavens receive my ghost, my corps I leave behind,
To be inclosd with his in earth, by those that shall it find.

Descend Providence.

Providence. Stay, stay thy stroke, thou wofull Dame, what 1550
wilt thou thus dispaire?

1526   distilled drops, for to bedew] bedewed drops, for to distill Q
1530   a sheepe] Dyce; as sheepe Q

Behold to let this wilfull fact, I *Providence* prepaire
To thee, from seate of mightie *Jove*, looke hereupon againe,
Reade, that if case thou canst it reade, and see if he be slaine
Whom thou doest love.   155
    Neronis. Ah heavens above,
All laud and praise and honour due, to you I here do render,
That would vouchsafe your handmaid here, in wofull state to
    tender:
By these same Verses do I find, my faithfull knight doth live,
Whose hand unto my deadly foe, the mortall stroke did give: 155
Whose cursed carkasse loe it is, which here on ground doth lie,
All honour due for this I yeeld, to mightie *Jove* on hie.
    Providence. Well, let desparation die in thee, I may not here
    remaine,
But be assured, that thou shalt ere long thy knight attaine.

Ascend.   156

    Neronis. And for their providence divine, the Gods above ile
    praise,
And shew their works so wonderfull, unto their laud alwaies.
[*sig. G1*]
Well, sith that the gods by providence hath signed unto mee
Such comfort sweete in my distresse, my Knight againe to see,
Farewell all feeding Shepherds flocks, unseemly for my state 157
To seeke my love I will set forth, in hope of friendly fate.
But first to Shepherds house I will, my pages tyre to take,
And afterwards depart from thence, my journey for to make.

Exit.   1573

[xix]

Enter Sir Clyomon.

    Clyomon. Long have I sought but all in vain, for neither far
    nor neare   157

1559 By] But by Q
1562 All] Ah Q

Of my *Neronis* wofull dame, by no meanes can I heare.
Did ever fortune violate two lovers in such sort?
The griefes all are intollerable, the which I do support
For want of her, but hope somewhat revives my pensive hart,
And doth to me some sodaine cause of comfort now impart   1580
Through newes I heare, as I abroad in weary travell went,
How that the Queene her mother hath her proclamations sent
Through every land, to get a Knight to combat on her side,
Against *Mustantius*, Duke and Lord, to have a matter tride:
And now the day is very nigh, as I do understand,   1585
In hope to meete my Lady there I will into that land:
And for her mother undertake the combat for to trye,
Yea though the other *Hector* were, I would him not denye
Whatsoever he be, but ere I go, a golden Sheeld ile have,
Although unknowne, I will come in, as doth my Knighthood crave: 1590
But covered will I keepe my Sheeld, because ile not be knowne,
If case my Lady be in place, till I have prowesse showne.
Well, to have my Sheeld in readinesse, I will no time delay,
And then to combat for the Queene, I straight will take my way.

                     Exit.   1595

                     [xx]

              Enter Neronis *like the Page.*

Neronis. Ah weary paces that I walke, with steps unsteddy
    still,
Of all the gripes of grislie griefes, *Neronis* hath her fill.
And yet amids these miseries, which were my first mishaps,
By brute I heare such newes alas, as more and more inwraps   1600
My wretched corps with thousand woes, more then I may support,
So that I am to be compared unto the scaled fort,
Which doth so long as men and might, and sustenance prevaile,
                                                   [*sig. G1v*]
Give to the enemies repulse, that commeth to assaile:
But when assistance gins to faile, and strength of foes increase, 1605

1578 all] ah Q

They forced are through battering blowes, the same for to release.
So likewise I so long as hope, my comfort did remaine,
The griesly greefes that me assaild, I did repulse againe:
But now that hope begins to faile, and greefes anew do rise,
I must of force yeeld up the Forte, I can no way devise   161(
To keepe the same, the Forte I meane, it is the wearie corse,
Which sorrowes daily do assaile, and siege without remorse:
And now to make my griefes the more, report alas hath told
How that my fathers aged bones, is shrined up in mold,
Since *Norway* king did me betray, and that my mother shee,   161:
Through Duke *Mustantius*, uncle mine, in great distresse to bee,
For swaying of the Septer there, what should I herein say?
Now that I cannot find my knight, I would at combat day
Be gladly there, if case I could with some good maister meete,
That as his Page in these affaires, would seeme me to intreate: 162(
And in good time, here commeth one, he seemes a knight to be,
Ile profer service, if in case, he will accept of me.

    Enter Clyomon *with his Sheeld covered, strangely disguised.*

    Clyomon. Well, now as one unknowne, I will go combat for
    the Queene:
Who can bewray me, since my Sheeld is not for to be seene? 162:
But stay, who do I here espie? of truth a proper Boy,
If case he do a maister lacke, he shall sustaine no noy:
For why in these affaires, he may stand me in passing steed.
    Neronis. Well, I see to passe upon my way, this Gentlemans
    decreed,
To him I will submit my selfe, in service for to be,   163(
If case he can his fancie frame, to like so well on me.
Well met sir knight upon your way.
    Clyomon. My Boy gramercies, but to me say,
Into what countrey is thy journey dight?
    Neronis. Towards the strange Marshes, of truth Sir Knight. 163:
    Clyomon. And thither am I going, high *Jove* be my guide.
    Neronis. Would Gods I were worthy to be your Page by your
    side.

1635 Marshes] Dyce; Marshe Q

Clyomon. My Page my boy, why what is thy name? that let
me heare.
Neronis. Sir Knight, by name I am called *Cur Daceer.* [*sig. G2*]
Clyomon. *Cur Daceer*, what heart of Steele, now certis my
boy, 1640
I am a Gentleman, and do entertaine thee with joy:
And to the strange Marshes am I going, the Queene to defend,
Come therefore, for without more saying, with me thou shalt wend.

Exit.

Neronis. As diligent to do my dutie as any in this land: 1645
Ah Fortune, how favourablie my friend doth she stand:
For thus no man knowing mine estate nor degree,
May I passe safely, a Page as you see.

Exit.

[xxi]

Enter Bryan sance toy with the [*Serpent's*] *Head.*

Bryan. Even as the Owle that hides her head, in hollow tree
till night,
And dares not while sir *Phoebus* shines, attempt abroad in flight: 1650
So likewise I as Buzzard bold, while chearefull day is seene,
Am forst with Owle to hire my selfe, amongst the Ivie greene:
And dares not with the seelie Snaile, from cabbin show my head, 1655
Till *Vesper* I behold aloft, in skies begin to spread:
And then as Owle that flies abroad when other fowles do rest,
I creepe out of my drowsie denne, when *Somnus* hath supprest
The head of everie valiant heart, loe thus I shrowd the day,
And travell as the Owle by night upon my wished way: 1660
The which hath made more tedious my journey, by halfe part,
But blame not *Bryan*, blame alas, his cowardly catiffes hart:
Which dares not showe it selfe by day, for feare of worthy wights,
For none can travell openly, to escape the venturous Knights,

1658 *Somnus*] Dyce; summous Q

Unlesse he have a noble mind, and eke a valiant hart,   1665
The which I will not brag upon, I assure you for my part:
For if the courage were in me, the which in other is,
I doubtles had injoyed the wight whom I do love ere this.
Well, I have not long to travel now, to *Denmarke* I draw nie,
Bearing knight *Clamydes* name, yet *Bryan sance foy* am I.   1670
But though I do usurpe his name, his sheeld or ensigne here,
Yet can I not usurpe his heart, still *Bryans* heart I beare:
Well, I force not that, he is safe inough, and *Bryan* as I am,
I will unto the Court, whereas I shall enjoy that dame.

Exit.   1675

[xxii]

[*sig. G2v*]

Enter Shift *like a Wiffler.*

Shift.   Rowme there for a reckning, see I beseech you if thale
    stand out of the way,
Jesu, Jesu, why do you not know that this is the day
That the combat must passe for *Mustantius* and the Queene?
But to fight upon her side as yet no Champion is seene.   1680
And Duke *Mustantius* he smiles in his sleeve, because he doth
    see
That neither for love nor rewards, any one her Champion will
    be.
Ant were not but that my maister the other Champion is,
To fight for the Queene my selfe, I surely would not mis.
Alas good Lady, she and her child is like to lose all the land,   1685
Because none will come in, in her defence for to stand.
For where she was in election, if any Champion had come
To rule till she was delivered, and have the Princes roome:
Now shall Duke *Mustantius* be sure the Scepter to sway,
If that none do come in to fight in her cause this day.   1690
And King *Alexander* all this while hath he stayed the triall to see,
Well here they come, roome for the King, heres such thrusting
of women as it grieveth mee.

Enter King Alexander, *the Queene,* Mustantius, *two Lords,*
        [*a Page*] *and* Clamydes *like a Champion.*   *1695*

Mustantius. O *Alexander* lo behold, before thy royall grace
My Champion here at pointed day I do present in place.
    Alexander. Well sir Duke in your defence is he content to be?
    Clamydes. Yea worthy Prince, not fearing who incounter shall
    with me:
Although he were with *Hercules* of cquall power and might,   1700
Yet in the cause of this same Duke, I challenge him the fight.
    Alexander. I like your courage well sir Knight: what shal we
    call your name?
    Clamydes. *Clamydes,* sonne to the *Swavian* King, O Prince
    so hight the same.
    Alexander. Now certainely I am right glad, *Clamydes* for to
    see,
Such valiant courage to remaine within the mind of thee.   1705
Well Lady, according to the order tane herein, what do you say,
Have you your Champion in like case, now ready at the day?
    Queene No sure, O King no Champion I have for to ayde
    my cause,
Unlesse twill please your noble grace an further day to pause.
For I have sent throughout this Ile, and every forraine land,   1710
But none as yet hath proffered, to take the same in hand. [*sig. G3*]
    Alexander. No, I am more sorie certainly, your chance to see
    so ill,
But day deferred cannot be, unlesse *Mustantius* will,
For that his Champion readie here, in place he doth present,
And who so missed at this day, should loose by full consent   1715
Of either part, the tytle right, and sway of regall Mace,
To this was your consentment given, as well as his in place,
And therefore without his assent, we cannot deferre the day.
    Shift. Ant shall please your grace, herein trie *Mustantius* what
    he will say.
    Alexander. How say you *Mustantius,* are you content the day
    to deferre?   1720

1709   an] on Q
1718   deferre] referre Q

Mustantius. Your Grace will not will me I trust, for then from
law you erre:
And having not her Champion here, according to decree,
There resteth nought for her to loose, the Crowne belongs to mee.
   Shift. Nay ant shall please your grace, rather then she shall it
   lose,
I my selfe will be her Champion for halfe a doozen blowes.   1725
   Mustantius. Wilt thou? then by full conge to the Challenger
   there stands.
   Shift. Nay soft, of sufferance commeth ease, though I cannot
rule my tongue, ile rule my hands.
   Mustantius. Well noble *Alexander*, sith that she wants her
Champion as you see,   1730
By greement of your royall grace, the Crowne belongs to mee.
   Alexander. Nay *Mustantius*, she shall have law, wherefore
   to sound begin,
To see if that in three houres space no Champion will come in.

                    Sound here once.

Of truth Madam I sorie am, none will thy cause maintaine,   1735
Well, according to the law of Armes, yet Trumpet sound againe.

                    Sound second time.

What, and is there none will take in hand, to Combat for the
   Queene?
   Shift. Faith I thinke it must be I must do the deed, for none
   yet is seene.
   Queene. O King let pittie pleade for me, here in your gracious
   sight,   1740
And for so slender cause as this deprive me not of right:
Consider once I had to spowse a Prince of worthy fame,
Though now blind Fortune spurne at me, her spight I needs must
   blame.

1726   conge] Bullen; congo Q

And though I am bereft O King, both of my child and mate,
Your Grace some greement may procure, consider of my state, 1745
And suffer not a Widow Queene with wrong oppressed so,
But pitie the young Infants case, wherewith O King I go:
                                                    [*sig. G3v*]
And though I suffer wrong, let that find favour in your sight.
 Alexander. Why Lady I respect you both, and sure would if I
 might
Entreate *Mustantius* thereunto, some such good order frame, 1750
Your strife should cease, and yet each one well pleased with the
 same.
 Queene. I know your grace may him perswade, as reason wils
 no lesse.
 Alexander. Well Sir *Mustantius,* then your mind to me in
 breefe expresse,
Will you unto such order stand here limited by me,
Without deferring longer time, say on if you agree? 1755
 Mustantius. In hope your grace my state will way, I give my
 glad consent.
 Alexander. And for to end all discord say, Madame, are you
 content?
 Queene. Yea noble King.
 Alexander. Well then before my nobles all, give eare unto the
 King,
For swaying of the sword and Mace all discord to beate downe, 1760
The child when it is borne, we elect to weare the Crowne.
And till that time *Mustantius,* you of lands and living heere,
Like equal part in everie point, with this the Queene shall share:
But to the child when it is borne, if Gods grant it to live,
The kingdome whole in every part, as tytle we do give. 1765
But yet *Mustantius,* we will yeeld this recompence to you,
You shall receive five thousand Crownes for yearely pension due,
To maintaine your estate, while you here live and do remaine,
And after let the whole belong unto the Crowne againe.
Now say your minds if you agree? 1770
 Page [*aside*]. I would the like choise were put to me.

1749 Alexander] speech prefixes in remainder of scene are King in Q

Mustantius. I for my part O Noble King therewith am well
content:

Queene. Well better halfe then nought at all, I likewise give
consent.

Enter Clyomon, as to Combat [and Neronis].

Clyomon. Renowned King and most of fame, before thy
royall grace,   1775
The Queene to aid, I do present my person here in place.

Mustantius. You come too late in faith Sir Knight, the houre
and time is past.

Clyomon. Your houre I am not to respect, I entered with
the blast.

Clamydes. What Princox is it you, are come to combat for
the Queene?

Good Fortune now, I hope ere long your courage shall be seene. 1780

Clyomon. And sure I count my hap as good, to meete with
you Sir knight.

Come according to your promise made, prepare your selfe to
fight.   [*sig. G4*]

Clamydes. ʾI knew you well inough sir, although your sheeld
were hid from mee.

Clyomon. Now you shall feele me as well as know me, if
hand and hart agree.   1785

Alexander. Stay, stay Sir knights, I charge you not in combat
to proceed,

For why the quarell ended is, and the parties are agreed:

And therefore we discharge you both, the combat to refraine:

Page. The heavens therefore O noble King, thy happie sheeld
remaine.

Clamydes. O King although we be dischargd for this contention now,   1790

Betwixt us twaine there resteth yet a combat made by vow

Which should be fought before your Grace: and since we here be
met

To judge twixt us for victorie, let me your Grace entreat.

1773   *Queene.*] assigned to Mustantius in Q

Alexander. For what occasion is your strife, sir knights first
let me know?

Clamydes. The trueth thereof renowned king thy servant he
shal show: 1795
What time O king, as I should take of *Suavia* king my sier,
The noble orders of a Knight, which long I did desier:
This knight a straunger comes to court, and at that present
   day,
In cowardly wise he comes by stealth, and takes from me away
The honour that I should have had, for which my father he,   1800
Did of his blessing give in charge, O noble king to me,
That I should know his name, that thus bereaved me of my right
The which he will not shew, unles he be subdued in fight:
Whereto we either plighted faith, that I should know his name,
If that before thy Grace O King, my force in fight could frame 1805
To vanquish him: now having met thus happily togither,
Though they are greed, our combat rests, decreed ere we came
   hither.

Alexander. Are you that knight that did subdue Sir *Samuel*
   in field,
For which you had in recompence of us, that Golden Sheeld?

Clyomon. I am that knight renowned Prince, whose name is
   yet unknowne,   1810
And since I foyld Sir *Samuel*, some prowesse I have showne.

Queene. Then as I gesse, you are that Knight by that same
   sheeld you bear,
Which sometime was restored to health within our Pallace here?
By *Neronis* our daughter, she betrayed by *Norway* king.

Clyomon. I am that knight indeed O Queene, whom she to
   health did bring,   1815
Whose servant ever I am bound wheresoever that she be,
Whose enemie O Queene is slaine pursuing her, by me. [*sig. G4v*]

Queene. Know you not where she abides, Sir knight to us
   declare?

1794   strife] Dyce; strifes Q
1807   rests] Dyce; rest Q
1808   *Alexander.*] Dyce; omitted in Q

Clyomon. No certis would to Gods I did, she should not live in care,
But escaped from the *Norway* king, I am assur'd she is.   1820
Queene. Well her absence was her fathers death, which turnd to bale my blis.
Clyomon. And till I find her out againe, my toile no end shall have.
Neronis [*aside*]. Alas he is nigh inough to her, small toile the space doth crave.
Alexander. Well Sir knights, since that you have declar'd before me here,   1825
The cause of this the grudge which you to each other beare:
I wish you both a while to pawse, and to my words attend,
If Reason rest with you, be sure Knights, this quarell I will end,
Without the sheading any bloud betwixt you here in fight:
Clamydes, wey you are nobly borne, and will you then sir Knight, 1830
Go hazard life so desperately? I charge you both refraine,
And since for so smal a cause, the strife doth grow betwixt you twaine:
And let him know your name sir knight, and so your malice end:
Clyomon. I have vowed to the contrary, which vowe I must defend.
Alexander. Well though so it be that you have vowed, your name shall not be knowne: 1835
Yet not detracting this your vow, your countrey may be showne,
And of what stocke by birth you bee:
Shift. Bur Lady he is dashed now I see.
Clyomon. Indeed this hath astond me much, I cannot but confesse,
My country and my birth, my state, which plainly wil expresse 1840
My name, for that unto them all my state is not unknowne.
Alexander. Sir knight, of our demand from you againe, what answere shall be showne?   1842b
Clyomon. Of *Denmarke* noble Prince I am, and son unto the king.

1823   *Neronis.*] Dyce; *Queene.* Q
1841   unknowne] Dyce; knowne Q

Alexander. Why then Sir *Cliomon* hight your name, as rare
report doth ring?

Clyomon. It doth indeed so hight my name, O Prince of high
renowne, 1845

I am the Prince of *Denmarkes* sonne, and heire unto the Crowne.

Clamydes. And are you son to *Denmarke* king? then do im-
brace your frend,

Within whose heart here towards you, all malice makes an end:

Who with your sister linked is, in love with loyall hart:

Clyomon. And for her sake, and for thine owne, like friendship I impart. 1850

Alexander. Well sir knights, since friendship rests, where
rancor did remaine,

And that you are such friends become, I certaine am right faine,

In hope you wil continue stil, you shall to Court repaire,

And remaine if that you please awhile, to rest you there [*sig. H1*]

Till time you have decreed which way your journey you will frame: 1855

Both. We yeeld you thanks, beseeching *Jove* still to augment
your fame.

Exeunt [Alexander *and his train*].

Clamydes. Well, come my *Clyomon* let us passe, and as we
journe by way,

My most misfortunes unto thee I wholly will bewray

What hapned in my last affaires, and for thy sisters sake. 1860

Clyomon. Well then *Cœur d'acer* come and waite, your journey you shall take,

And seeing thou art prepared, and hast all things in readinesse,

Hast thee before to *Denmarke* with speedinesse,

And tell the King and the Queene that *Clyomon* their sonne

In health and happie state to their court doth returne. 1865

Clamydes. But in no wise to *Juliana* say any thing of mee.

Neronis. I will not shew one word amisse contrary your decree.

Clamydes. Well then my *Clyomon*, to take our leave to court
let us repare:

1866 *Clamydes.*] Bullen; omitted in Q
1867 *Neronis.*] *Curdaser.* Q

Clyomon. As your friend and companyon *Clamydes* every where.

Exit.   1869b

Neronis. Oh heavens! is this my loving knight whom I have
servd so long?   1870
Now have I tride his faithfull hart, oh so my joyes doth throng,
To thinke how Fortune favoreth me, *Nerones* now be glad,
And praise the gods, thy journey now, such good successe hath
had.
To *Denmarke* will I hast with joy my message to declare,
And tell the King how that his sonne doth homeward now repaire. 1875
And more to make my joyes abound, Fortune could never frame
A finer meane to serve my turne, then this, for by the same
I may unto the Queene declare my state in secret wise,
And by the way I will recount how best I can devise.
Now pack *Nerones* like a page, hast hence lest thou be spide,   1880
And tell thy maisters message there, the gods my journey guide.

Exit.   1881b

[xxiii]

Enter King of Denmarke, *the Queene,* Juliana, *two Lords.*

King. Come Lady Queene, and daughter eke, my *Juliana*
deare,
We muse that of your Knight as yet no newes againe you heare,
Which did adventure for your love the Serpent to subdue.   1885
    Juliana. O father, the sending of that worthy knight my woful
hart doth rue,
For that alas the furious force of his outragious might,
As I have heard subdued hath full many a worthy knight.
And this last night O father past, my mind was troubled sore,
Me thought in dreame I saw a Knight not knowne to me before, 1890
[*sig. H1v*]
Which did present to me the head of that same monster slaine,
But my *Clamydes* still in voyce me thought I heard complaine,

As one bereft of all his joy, now what this dreame doth signifie,
My simple skill will not suffice the truth thereof to specifie.
But sore I feare to contraries, the exspect thereof will hap,   1895
Which will in huge calamities my wofull corps bewrap:
For sending of so worthy a Prince, as was *Clamydes* he,
To sup his dire destruction there, for wretched love of me.
    Queene. Tush daughter these but fancies be, which run within
your mind:
    King. Let them for to suppresse your joyes, no place of har- 1900
bour find.
    Lord. O Princes let no dollors dant, behold your Knight in
place:
    Juliana. Ah happie sight, do I behold my knight Clamydes
face?

    Enter Bryan Sance foy *with the head on his sword.*

    Bryan. Wel, I have at last through travell long, atchived my
journeys end,
Though *Bryan*, yet *Clamydes* name, I stoutly must defend.   1905
Ah happie sight, the King and Queene with daughter in like case
I do behold, to them I will present my selfe in place:
The mightie Gods renowmed King, thy princely state maintaine:
    King. Sir *Clamydes*, most welcome sure you are to court
againe.
    Bryan. O Princes lo my promise here performed thou maist
see,   1910
The Serpents head by me subdude I do present to thee,
Before thy fathers royall grace:
    Juliana. My *Clamydes* do embrace
Thy *Juliana*, whose hart thou hast till vitall race be runne:
Sith for her sake so venturously this deed by thee was done.   1915
Ah welcome home my faithfull Knight:
    Bryan. Gramerces noble Lady bright.
    King. Well *Juliana* in our court your lover cause to stay,
For all our Nobles we will send, against your nuptiall day.
Go cary him to take his rest: 1920
    Juliana. I shall obey your graces hest.

Come my *Clamydes* go with me, in court your rest to take:
Bryan. I thanke you Lady, now I see accompt of me you make.

Exeunt.

King. Well my Queene, sith daughter ours hath chosen such 1925
a make,
The terrour of whose valiant hart may cause our foes to quake,
[*sig. H2*]
Come let us presently depart, and as we did decree,
For all our nobles will we send, their nuptialls for to see.
Queene. As pleaseth thee, thy Lady Queene O king is well
agreed.
Lord. May it please your graces to arest, for loe with posting
speed   1930
A messenger doth enter place:
King. Then will we stay to know the case.

Enter Neronis.

Neronis. The mightie powers renowned Prince preserve your
state for ay.
King. Messenger thou art welcome, what hast thou to say?   1935
Neronis. Sir *Clyomon* your noble sonne, knight of the golden
Sheeld,
Who for his valiant victories in Towne and eke in field
Is famed through the world, to your court doth now returne,
And hath sent me before to Court, your grace for to enforme.
King. Ah messenger declare, is this of truth the which that 1940
thou hast told?
Neronis. It is most true O Noble king, you may thereof be
bold.
King. Ah joy of joyes surpassing all, what joy is this to me?
My *Clyomon* in Court to have, the nuptiall for to see,
Of *Juliana* sister his, oh so I joy in mind.
Queene. My boy where is thy maister speake, what is he far
behind?   1945
Declare with speed, for these my eyes do long his face to view:

Neronis. Oh Queene this day he will be here, tis truth I tell to
you.
But noble Queene let pardon here my bold attempt excuse,
And for to heare a simple boy in secret not refuse,
Who hath strange tidings from your sonne to tell unto your grace. 1950

Exit [*with Queene*]. 1950b

Lord. Behold my Lord where as I gesse, some strangers enter
place:
King. I hope my *Clyomon* be not far, Oh joy, I see his face.

[*Enter* Clyomon, Clamydes, *and* Shift.]

Clyomon. Come Knowledge, come forward, why art thou al-
waies slacke?
Get you to Court, brush up our apparell, untrusse your packe:
Go seeke out my Page, bid him come to me with all speed you can: 1955
Shift. Go seek out, fetch, bring here, gogs ounds, what am I,
a dog or a man?
I were better be a hangman, and live so like a drudge:
Since your new man came to you, I must packe, I must trudge.
Clyomon. How stands thou knave? why gets thou not away?
Shift. Now, now sir, you are so hastie now, I know not what
to say. 1960
Clyomon. O noble Prince, the Gods above preserve thy royall
grace:
King. How joyfull is my heart deare sonne, to view againe thy
face? [*sig. H2v*]
Clyomon. And I as joyfull in the view of parents happie
plight,
Whom sacred gods long time maintaine in honor day and night.
But this my friend O father deere, even as my selfe intreate 1965
Whose noblenes when time shall serve to you he shall repeate.
King. If case my sonne he be thy friend, with hart I thee im-
brace:
Clamydes. With loyall hart in humble wise, I thanke your
noble grace. 1968

1968 *Clamydes.*] Dyce; *Clyomon.* Q

King. My *Clyomon* declare my sonne in thine adventures late,
What hath bin wrought by Fortune most to advance thy noble
state?   1970
Clyomon. O father, the greatest joy of the joyes which was to
one assignd
Since first I left your noble court, by cruell Fortune blind,
Is now bereft from me away, through her accursed fate,
So that I rather finde she doth envy my noble state,
Then seeke for to advance the same, so that I boldly may   1975
Expresse she never gave so much, but more she tooke away,
And that which I have lost by her, and her accursed ire,
From travell will I never cease untill I may aspire
Unto the view thereof oh King, wherein is all my joy.
 King. Why how hath Fortune wrought to thee this care and
great anoy?   1980
 Clyomon. O father unto me the heavenly power assignd a
noble dame,
With whome to live in happy life, my hart did wholie frame.
But not long did that glasing starre, give light unto mine eyes,
But this fell Fortune gins to frowne, which every state despise
And takes away through cancred hate that happy light from me, 1985
In which I fixed had my hope, a blessed state to see:
And daughter to the King she was, which of strange Marshes
hight,
Bearing brute each where, to be dame Bewties darling bright:
Right heire unto dame Vertues grace, dame Natures patterne true,
Dame Prudence scholler for her wit, dame *Venus* for her hue. 1990
Diana for her daintie life, *Susanna* being sad,
Sage *Saba* for her sobernesse, mild *Martha* being glad.
And if I should reentre make, amongst the Muses nine,
My Lady lackt no kind of art, which man may well define
Amongst those daintie dames to be: then let all judge that heare, 1995
If that my cause it be not just, for which this pensive cheare
Fell Fortune forceth me to make.
 King. Yet *Clyomon* good counsell take.   [*sig. H3*]
Let not the losse of the Lady thine so pinch thy hart with griefe,

1992   *Martha*] Bullen; *Marpha* Q

That nothing may unto thy mind give comfort or reliefe: 2000
What man there Ladies are enow, although that she be gone,
Then leave to waile the want of her, cease off to make this mone.
   Clyomon. No father, never seeme for to perswade, for as is
said before,
What travell I have had for her, it shall be tryple more,
Untill I meete with her againe. 2005
   Clamydes. Well *Clyomon*, a while refraine,
And let me here my woes recount before your fathers grace
But let me crave, your sister may be sent for into place.
O King vouchsafe I may demaund a simple bound,
Although a straunger, yet I hope such favour may be found: 2010
The thing is this, that you will send for *Juliana* hither,
Your daughter faire, that we may talke a word or twaine togither.
   King. For what, let me know sir knight, do you her sight
desire?
   Clyomon. The cause pretends no harme my Liege, why he
doth this require.
   King. My Lord go bid our daughter come and speake with
me straight way. 2015
   Lord. I shall my Liege in everie point, your mind herein
obey.

Exit.   2016b

   Clyomon. O father this is *Clamydes*, and sonne to *Swavia*
King,
Who for my sister ventured life, the serpents head to bring:
With whom I met in travell mine, but more what did befall,
To worke his woe when as she comes your grace shall know it all. 2020
   King. My sonne you are deceived much, I you assure in this,
The person whom you tearme him for, in court alreadie is.
   Clyomon. No father I am not deceived, this is *Clamydes*
sure.
   King. Well my sonne do cease a while such talke to put in
ure:
For loe thy sister entereth place, which soone the doubt shall end. 2025

2023 *Clyomon.*] Dyce; *Clamy.* Q

Clamydes. Then for to shew my name to her, I surely do
pretend.

Enter Juliana.

My *Juliana* noble Dame, *Clamydes* do embrace,
Who many a bitter brunt hath bode, since that he saw thy face.
Juliana. Avaunt dissembling wretch, what credit canst thou
yeeld?   2030
Wher's the serpents head thou brought, where is my glittering
Sheeld?
Tush, tush sir knight, you counterfet, you would *Clamydes* be,
But want of these bewraies you quite, and shewes you are not he.
Clamydes. O Princes do not me disdaine, I certaine am your
knight: [*sig. H3v*]
Juliana. What art thou franticke foolish man? avaunt from
out my sight.   2035
If thou art he, then shew my sheeld, and bring the Serpents head:
Clamydes. O Princesse heare me shew my case, by Fortuné
fell decreed.
I am your Knight, and when I had subdued the monster fell,
Through wearie fight and travell great, as Knowledge here can
tell:
I laid me downe to rest a space within the Forrest, where   2040
One *Bryan* that *Sance foy* hight, who with cowardly usage there,
By chaunting charme, brought me a sleepe, then did he take
from me
The Serpents head, my coate and sheeld, the which you gave
to me:
And left me in his prison loe, still sleeping as I was.

*   *   *

Loe Lady thus I lost those things the which to me you gave,   2045
But certainly I am your Knight, and he who did deprave

2027   *Enter . . .*] l. 2029 in Q
2030   *Juliana.*] omitted in Q
2041   that] than Q

The flying Serpent of his life according as you willed,
That who so wonne your love by him, the same should be ful-
filled.
   Juliana. Alas poore knight, how simplie have you framed this
excuse?
The name of such a noble knight to usurpe and eke abuse.   2050
   Clyomon. No sister you are deceived, this is *Clamydes* sure:
   Juliana. No brother, then you are deceived, such tales to put
in ure:
For my *Clamydes* is in Court, who did present to me,
In white attire the Serpents head and Sheeld, as you do see.
   Clamydes. That shall I quickly understand, O king permit I
may   2055
Have conference a while with him, whom as your grace doth say,
Presents *Clamydes* for to be, before your royall grace:
   Juliana. Behold no whit agast to shew himselfe, where he doth
enter place.

[*Enter* Bryan]

   Clamydes. Ah traytor, art thou he that doth my name and
state abuse?
   Juliana. Sir knight you are too bold in presence here, such   2060
talke against him for to use.
   Bryan. Wherefore doest thou upbraid me thus, thou varlet do
declare?
   Clyomon. No varlet he, to call him so, sir knight you are too
blame:
   Clamydes. Wouldst thou perstand for what intent such talk
I here do frame?
Because I know thou doest usurpe my state and noble name.   2065
   Bryan. Who art thou, or whats thy name? reanswere quickly
make:
   Clamydes. I am *Clamydes*, whose name to beare, thou here
doest undertake.
   Bryan. Art thou *Clamydes?* vaunt thou false usurper of my
state,

2054 as you do see] as yet to see Q

Avoyd this place, or death shall be thy most accursed fate.

[*sig. H4*]

How darest thou enterprise to take my name thus unto thee?
Clamydes. Nay rather, how darest thou attempt to usurpe
the name of me?   2071
Juliana. You lie Sir Knight, he doth not so, gainst him you
have it done.
Clyomon. Sister you are deceived, my frind here is *Clamydes*
Prince, the King of *Suavias* sonne.
Juliana. Nay Brother, neither you nor he can me deceive
herein.   2075

*   *   *

Clamydes. O King bowe downe thy princely eares, and listen
what I say,
To prove my selfe the wight I am before your royall grace,
And to disprove this faithlesse Knight which here I find in place,
For to usurpe my name so much, the combat will I trie:
For before I will mine honour loose, I rather chuse to die.   2080
King. I like well your determined mind, but how say you sir
knight?
Shift. Nay by his ounds ile gage my gowne he dares not fight:
Bryan. By gogs bloud I shall be slaine now, if the Combat I
denie,
And not for the eares of my head with him I dare trie.
King. Sir knight why do you not reanswere make in triall of
your name?   2085
Bryan. I will O King, if case he dare in combat trie the same.
King. Well then go to prepare your selves, each one his
weapons take:
Juliana. Good father let it not be so, restraine them for my
sake.
I may not here behold my Knight in daunger for to be,
With such a one who doth usurpe his name to purchase me: 2090
I speake not this for that I feare his force or strength in fight,

2082   *Shift.*] Bullen; *Bryan.* in Q
2083   *Bryan.*] Bullen; omitted in Q

But that I will not have him deale with such a desperate wight.

    King. Nay sure, there is not better way then that which is
decreed,

And therefore for to end their strife the combat shall proceed:

Sir Knights prepare your selves, the truth thereof to trie.   2095

    Clamydes. I readie am, no cowardly heart shall cause me to
denie.

    Bryan. Nay ile never stand the triall of it, my heart to fight
doth faint:

Therefore ile take me to my legs, seeing my honour I must
attaint.

    King. Why wither runs *Clamydes?* Sir knight seeme to stay
him:

    Clyomon. Nay it is *Clamydes* O King that doth fray him.   2100

    Clamydes. Nay come sir come, for the combat we will trie:

    Bryan. Ah no my heart is done, to be *Clamydes* I denie.

    King. Why how now *Clamydes*, how chance you do the com-
bat here thus shunne?

    Bryan. Oh King grant pardon unto me, the thing I have be-
gunne   2105

I must denie, for I am not *Clamides*, this is plaine: [*sig. H4v*]

Though greatly to my shame, I must my words revoke againe:

I am no other then the knight, whome they *Sance Foy* call,

This is *Clamydes*, the feare of whom, my danted mind doth pall.

    Juliana. Is this *Clamydes?* ah worthy Knight, then do for-
give thy deere,   2110

And welcome eke ten thousand times unto thy Lady heere.

    Clamydes. Ah my *Juliana* bright, whats past I do forgive,

For well I see thou constant art, and whilst that I do live,

For this, my firmed faith in thee for ever ile repose.

    Juliana. O father now I do deny that wretch, and do amongst 2115
my foes

Recount him for this treason wrought.

    King. Well Knowledge, take him unto thee, and for the small
regard

The which he had to valiant Knights, this shalbe his reward,

Sith he by charmes, his crueltie in cowardly manner wrought,

On Knights, who as *Clamydes* did, the crowne of honour sought, 2120
An trayterously did them betray, in prison for to keepe,
The fruits of such like crueltie, himselfe by us shall reape:
By due desert therefore I charge to prison him convay,
There for to lye perpetually unto his dying day.
   Bryan. Oh King be mercifull, and shew some favour in this
case: 2125
   King. Nay, never thinke that at my hands thou shalt finde
any grace.

[*Exit* Bryan *and* Shift.]

Clamydes, ah most welcome thou, our daughter to enjoy,
The heavens be praisd that this hath wrought, to foile all future
noy.
   Clamydes. I thanke your Grace, that you thus so well esteeme
of me.

*   *   *

[*Enter* Shift.]

   Shift. What is all things finished, and every man eased? 2130
Is the pageant packed up, and all parties pleased?
Hath each Lord his Lady, and each Lady her love?
   Clyomon. Why Knowledge, what meanst thou those motions
to move?
   Shift. You were best stay a while, and then you shall know,
For the Queene her selfe comes, the motion to show. 2135
You sent me if you remember, to seeke out your page,
But I cannot find him, I went whisling and calling through the
court in such a rage:
At the last very scacely in at a chamber I did pry,
Where the Queene with other Ladyes very busy I did spy:
Decking up a strange Lady very gallant and gay, 2140
To bring her here in presence, as in court I heard say.
   Clyomon. A strange Lady Knowledge, of whence is she canst
thou tell me?

2130 *Shift.*] Dyce; *Enter Knowledge.* Q
2134 *Shift.*] Dyce; *Knowledge.* Q.

Shift. Not I ant shall please you, but anon you shall see.

[*sig. I1*]

For lo where the Lady with your mother doth come.

[*Enter Queene and* Neronis.]

Clyomon. Then straightway my duty to her grace shalbe
done. 2145

The mighty Gods preserve your state, O Queene, and mother
deare,

Hoping your blessing I have had, though absent many a yeare.

Queene. My *Clyomon*, thy sight my son doth make thy aged
mother glad,

Whose absence long and many a yeare, hath made thy pensive
parents sad.

And more to let thee know my sonne, that I do love and tender
thee, 2150

I have here for thy welcome home, a present which ile give to
thee.

This Lady though she be unknowne, refuse her not, for sure her
state

Deserves a Princes sonne to wed, and therefore take her for thy
mate.

Clyomon. O noble Queene and mother deere, I thanke you
for your great good will,

But I am otherwise bestowd, and sure I must my oath fulfill. 2155

And so I mind if gods to fore, on such decree I meane to pause,

For sure I must of force deny, my noble father knowes the cause.

King. Indeed my Queene this much he told, he lov'd a Lady
since he went,

Who hath his hart and ever shall, and none but her to love he's
bent.

Clyomon. So did I say, and so I wil, no beawties blaze, no
glistering wight. 2160

Can cause me to forget her love, to whom my faith I first did
plight.

2143　*Shift.*] Dyce; *Knowledge.* Q
2148　*Queene.*] Dyce; *Enter Queene.* Q

Neronis. Why are you so straight lac't sir Knight, to cast a Lady off so coy?

Turne once againe and looke on me, perhaps my sight may bring you joy.

Clyomon. Bring joy to me? alas which way? no Ladies looks can make me glad:

Neronis. Then were my recompence but small, to quit my paine for you I had.   2165

Wherefore sir knight do wey my words, set not so light the love I show,

But when you have bethought your selfe, you wil recant and turne I know.

Queene. My *Clyomon* refuse her not, she is and must thy Lady be:

Clyomon. If otherwise my mind be bent, I trust your grace will pardon me.

Neronis. Wel then I see tis time to speake, sir knight let me   2170 one question crave.

Clyomon. Say on your mind.

Neronis. Where is that Lady now become, to whom your plighted faith you gave?

Clyomon. Nay if I could absolve that doubt, then were my mind at ease:

Neronis. Were you not brought to health by her, when you came sick once of the seas?

Clyomon. Yea sure I must confesse a truth, she did restore my health to me,   2175

For which good deed I rest her owne, in hope one day her face to see.

Neronis. But did you not promise her to returne, to see her at a certaine day,

And ere you came that to performe, the *Norway* King stole her away?

And so your Lady there you lost:

Clyomon. All this I graunt, but to his cost   2180

2171 *Clyomon.*] Dyce; omitted in Q
2172 *Neronis.*] Dyce; omitted in Q

For stealing her against her will, this hand of mine bereft his life.

[*sig. 11v*]

Neronis. Now sure sir knight you servd him wel, to teach
him know an other mans wife:

But yet once more sir Knight replie, the truth I crave to understand,

In Forrest once, who gave you drink, whereas you stood with
sword in hand,

Fearing least some had you pursude for sleying of your enemie? 2185

Clyomon. That did a sillie shepheards boy, which there I tooke
my Page to be.

Neronis. And what is of that Page become, remains he with
you, yea or no?

Clyomon. I sent him hither ere I came, because the King and
Queene should know,

That I in health returned was, but since I never saw him.

Neronis. And sure he stands not far from hence, though now
you do not know him. 2190

Clyomon. Not far from hence, where might he be?

Neronis. Of troth Sir Knight, my selfe am he:

I brought your message to the King, as here the Queene can
testifie:

I gave you drinke in Forrest sure, when you with drought were
like to die.

I found you once upon the shore full sicke, when as you came
from seas. 2195

I brought you home to fathers Court, I sought al means your
mind to pleas,

And I it was that all this while have waighted like a Page on thee:

Still hoping for to spie a time wherein I might discover mee.

And so by hap at last I did, I thanke your mothers noble grace:

She entertaind me courteously, when I had told her all my case. 2200

And now let this suffice my deare, I am *Neronis* whom you see,

Who many a wearie step hath gone, before and since I met with
thee.

Clyomon. O sudden joyes, O heavenly sight, O words more
worth then gold,

Neronis, O my deare welcome, my armes I here unfold,
To clasp thy comely corps withall, twice welcome to thy knight. 220
   Neronis. And I as joyfull am no doubt, my *Clyomon* of thy
   happie sight.
   Clyomon. Clamydes my assured friend, lo how Dame Fortune
   favoreth mee,
This is *Neronis* my deare love, whose face so long I wisht to see.
   Clamydes. My *Clyomon,* I am as glad as you your selfe to
   see this day:
   King. Well daughter though a stranger yet, welcome to Court
   as I may say. 221
   Queene. And Lady as welcome unto me, as if thou wert mine
   onely child.
   Neronis. For this your gracious curtesie, I thanke you noble
   Princes mild.
   Juliana. Thogh strange and unacquainted yet, do make ac-
   count you welcome are,
Your nuptiall day as well as mine, I know my father will prepare.
   King. Yes we are prest your nuptiall day with daughter ours
   to see, 221:
As well as *Clyomons* our sonne, with this his Lady faire:
Come therefore to our Court, that we the same may soone pre-
   pare.
For we are prest throughout our land, for all our Peeres to send:
   Omnes. Thy pleasure most renowned King, thy servants shall
   attend.

Finis.

NOTES

The Prologue

1 *worthy writers workes:* presumably *Perceforest,* his source. The appeal in the Prologue to the finer taste of the "Courteous" and "gentle" may not be entirely rhetorical since the quarto may have been designed with a view toward upper-class buyers. Charles C. Mish suggests that the cleavage in the reading public between upper-class taste for sentimental and heroic romances and middle class taste for chivalric romances is reflected by a fairly consistent and distinctive typography – roman type for the upper-class romances (the type of *Clyomon and Clamydes* quarto) and black-letter for middle-class romances ("Black Letter as a Social Discriminate in the Seventeenth Century", *PMLA* [1953], 627-630).

3 *acts and deeds ... lurks:* The use of the *-s* plural of verbs (e.g. *makes seemes*) and of *doth, hath* and *is* with plural subjects may be considered normal for the text, and I have not commented on them (Wyld, p. 340; Abbott, p. 333).

8-12 *Wherein:* anaphora, or "Report according to the Greeke originall, and is when we make one work begin, as they are wont to say, lead the daunce to many verses in sute ..." (Puttenham, p. 208).

11 *facts:* evil or ignominous acts. The word appears four times in the text, each time in this sense. Cf. "alasse is my fact so heinous that none will pitie me?" (*True*

Tragedie, ll. 1131-32); "Tis incest and too fowle a fact for kings" (*Looking Glass,* l. 116).

11 *ignomius:* ignominious. Cf. the contraction ignomy at ll. 253 ("let ignomy to my reproach") and 891 ("to me the blast of ignomy") and in *Measure for Measure,* II, iv. 111 and *1 Henry IV,* V. iv. 100.

14 *doubting:* fearing.

15 *prest:* ready (cf. French prêt).

16 *frustrate:* (adj.) fruitless, unavailing. Cf. "Nay lady he that talkes with you vntill the field he gaine / Should proue the labour he should take both frustrate, fond and vain" (*Conditions,* ll. 831-32).

16 *to whom*: as regards (about) whom (Abbott, p. 188).

scene i

scene i: Clamydes' meeting with Juliana is based on *Perceforest* II, 33 and 42. The extensive alterations of the source are noted in the introduction (pp. 40-44).

2-36 The petrarchan image of the mariner who has passed through the storms of love to arrive safely at the harbor of the lady's mercy derives ultimately from Ariosto's "O sicuro, secreto e fidel porto", *Lirica,* no. 3. The playwright's use of the image here and again at ll. 1056-64 is apparently both literal and figurative.

2 *waltring waves:* a standard alliterative phrase. See *Patience,* l. 142, Barbour's *Bruce,* III, 699-700 and 719 and *The Misfortunes of Arthur,* II, iii, 153 and III, Chorus, 42.

8 *Clamydes:* normally accented on the second syllable though in a few lines the meter requires that the first syllable be accented.

8 *Swavia noble soyle:* The playwright regularly uses proper nouns as possessive adjectives. On the freedom with which one part of speech was used as another, see Abbott, pp. 22 and 430.

16 *For why:* therefore.

16 *doubtfull:* dreadful, fearful.

17 *bearing lesser braine:* being less cautious; (as in *Grim the Collier*, V. i. 1-2 (Dodsley, vol. 8); or perhaps being less sensible, as in *All Fools*, IV, i. 204 (ed. T. M. Parrott, 1907).

18 *travell:* travail.

21 *custome:* feudal rent.

21 *taske:* any fixed feudal payment, tax, tribute.

22 *meane by:* mean. So Puttenham, quoting his lines on Elizabeth, says "any simple iudgement might easily perceive by whom it was ment, that is by Lady Elizabeth. . . ." (Puttenham, p. 203). The playwright's explication of his metaphor here and elsewhere is termed by Puttenham "mixed" allegory because he explains that "which in a full allegorie should not be discouered, but left at large to the readers judgement and coniecture" (Puttenham, p. 198).

22 *Juliana she:* a common rhetorical embellishment in the play, iteration of the pronoun after proper nouns, personifications and, occasionally, after strongly emphasized epithets (Abbott, p. 243).

37 *white Sheeld:* Cf. *Perceforest* II, 144, where Bethides is called "le Blanc Chevalier" "pource quil porta au tournoy [given in connection with the knighting ceremony] blanches armes sans autre enseigne". Lyonnel du Glar receives a different shield from a maiden sent by Blanche, a shield bearing on one side a portrait of the lady and on the other, a portrait of the Giant with the Golden Hair (II, 42).

41 *forge:* deceive.

44 *In mids:* a variant of ME. amiddes, imyddes (amidst) (O.E.D.).

45 *perstand:* apparently a combination of *perceive* and *understand* (O.E.D.). The playwright's freedom with prefixes in this and in *prepare* (repair), *pretend* (intend) and *prevail* (avail) is approved by Puttenham as one of

the "auricular figures" whose purpose is to alter "the tune and harmonie of a meeter as to the eare" (Puttenham, p. 173).

47-52 In his compression of his source, the playwright transfers the flying serpent from an unspecified island to the Forest of Marvels and the enmity of Darnant and the "mauvais lignage" for all womankind (volume I) to the flying serpent.

60 *brute:* i.e. bruit.

62 *Serbarus:* Cerberus, like Curdaser and Cur Daceer later in the text, phonetic spellings that may have originated with a scribe.

71 *For why:* because.

83 *elevate:* magnify (O.E.D. 5, b).

94 *prepare:* repair. See note 45.

97 *Tyger fell and Monster fierce:* Perhaps indication of revision (see introduction, p. 18m.) or simply a loose end carried over from the source. Lyonnel du Glar undertakes the quest of the Giant with the Golden Hair, but before he arrives in the land dominated by the giant, he encounters and slays two lions that are ravaging the Kingdom of the Strange Marches and a flying serpent that is spreading terror among the mariners (II, 42-44, 58). In *Perceforest* the lion represents Christ and the serpent "l'Escriture mauvaisement entendue" but in the play the symbolic significance is lost (See Lods, p. 62).

97 *dint:* dealing blows, force (O.E.D. 2).

102 *travels:* travail's.

105-6 *booted:* Both Clyomon and Shift are "booted", i.e. dressed for travel.

106 *Shift:* a double-dealer, one who lives by fraud and deceit, the most characteristic feature of the Vice. Compare Ambodexter, the Vice of *Cambises,* and Hardydardy, the Vice of *Godly Queen Hester,* whose names denote the same quality. E.g. Edricus' claim in *Edmond Ironsides,* "Yet can I play an Ambodexters part? And sweare I love, yet hate him with my harte" and Shift's

statement that "such shifting knaves as I am, the Ambodexter must play" (l. 633). Hardy-dardy, the name for the children's game of guess in which hand a coin is hidden, also implies "double-crossing" or "ambidexterity" (see A. P. Rossiter, *English Drama from Early Times to the Elizabethans* [London, 1950], p. 126).

106 *the Vice:* a theatrical rather than literary term designating vice characters who appear confusingly under several names. (Shift appears as Knowledge, Shift, Ambodexter, Policy.) The term was first used as a proper noun in Heywood's *Play of the Wether* (1533) and appears subsequently in players' lists and stage directions of 20 plays surviving from the sixteenth century. (See L. W. Cushman, *The Devil and the Vice in the English Dramatic Literature Before Shakespeare* [Halle, 1900], pp. 67-88) For a discussion of Subtle Shift as a Vice character, see introduction pp. 49-52.

110 *ant:* and it, if it. Shift's tag line "ant shall please" occurs 23 times in the play.

112 *beraide:* befouled.

scene ii

118-120 See introduction, p. 35. Cf. Shift's stage business and the appropriation of the theater doors for dramatic purposes with the direction "Ionas the Prophet cast out of the Whales belly vpon the Stage" (*Looking Glass*, 1460-61).

135 *it skils not:* It makes no difference.

147 *say nay and take it:* "Maids say nay and take it" (Tilley, M 34). Cf. *Richard III*, III. vii. 51; *Looking Glass*, ll. 473-4. Though the play is not rich in proverbial expressions, it follows the customary practise of assigning the proverbs to comic characters. (Whiting, pp. 209ff.) Thus Shift is assigned four proverbs, Bryan and Corin

one each. Of the two remaining proverbs, one is assigned to Neronis and one to Mustantius.

152 *arrant:* errand. Here with the connotation of dignity,
elevation – a mission (O.E.D., 2, a).

166-181 Shift's exit provides the opportunity for Clyomon's
speech celebrating the glories of war. Unlike the set-
speech on the duties of knighthood in the succeeding
scene, it does not draw from the details of *Perceforest.*

169 *haughtie:* high-minded, aspiring, here without the connotation of arrogance.

169 *imploy:* devote (O.E.D. 1, b).

174 *then:* than (i.e. "Can musicke . . . delight, Can comfort
. . . Rejoyce the pensive and carefull [more] then. . . ."

181 *auncients:* ensigns, flags.

215 *to be lost:* i.e. lose the tournament.

scene iii

scene iii: from *Perceforest* II, 143, where Perceforest, King of
Great Britain, holds a feast celebrating his return to
health and a tournament celebrating the knighting of
his son Bethides and of two nephews. Perceforest's
speech on the duties of knighthood takes up an entire
chapter. The knighting scene follows the source with
great fidelity.

223 *prest:* ready.

257 *den of darksomenesse:* apparently a common alliterative
phrase. Cf. "darksome den" in *Apius and Virginia,* l.
616.

258 *prefers:* promotes.

261 *place:* (usually "the place") or *platea,* from medieval
times a technical theatrical term designating the open
area – a public square, a green – upon which "scaf-
folds" were erected. Though "the place" included the
acting area, it was primarily the "area on which the
audience stood before a raised stage or stages (c. 1146

to c. 1516(?))." Richard Southern, *The Medieval Theatre in the Round* (London, 1957), pp. 17-142. For the use of the term in sixteenth-century plays see Chambers III, 22, n 5; 37, n 3. The term appears in *Clyomon and Clamydes* in this single stage direction, but it occurs frequently in the text – particularly in the last pages – to indicate entrances (e.g. "behold your knight in place", "a messenger doth enter place", "some strangers enter place", "loe thy sister entereth place"). The playwright apparently uses the term here to designate the theatrical area in general while "stage", which appears in the direction at l. 118, he uses to designate the platform itself.

268 *Hardie:* bold. So *Perceforest:* "Chevalier soyes preux et hardy et loyal. . . ."

272 *tane:* taken. Like *paraunter* for *parauenter, poorety* for *pouerty,* and *souraigne* for *soueraigne,* an example of the omission of a letter of syllable ("rabbating") in order to alter the meter or to provide a rhyme. (See Abbott, p. 148; Puttenham, p. 173).

273 *Pursue him:* probably an addition made by the bookkeeper. Q reads *Pursue him, and bring in* Shift. Though it duplicates the direction at ll. 281-2, presumably the author's, this first direction is an exit while the second is an entrance.

275 *meere:* total, complete. Cf. *Grissell,* l. 1861; *Othello,* II, ii. 3.

284 *prevaileth:* availeth. See 45n.

286 *grudge:* injury (O.E.D. 5).

294 *should have bene:* was to have been.

303-4 *force of hand Or love:* Cf. *Perceforest* "par force ou paramour".

320 *dinted:* violent. A figurative extension of to dint – to strike, beat, knock (O.E.D. 1).

324 *retire:* return, come back.

325 *ayder:* Dyce emends to plural, but similar constructions appear at ll. 385 and 655.

326 *hire:* reward.

327 *pretend:* intend. See 45n. Cf. also *Conditions*, 1. 106. "If that thou retourne, thy death is pretended."

330 *tend:* attend. Cf. *signed* (assigned), *tempt* (attempt), *pointed* (appointed), *gratulation* (congratulation). Another example of "rabbating" whereby an author may "alter his wordes, and sometimes it is done for pleasure to giue a better sound, sometimes vpon necessitie, and to make vp the rime" (Puttenham, p. 174). Many of these forms suggest that the prefixes were omitted in pronunciation (Abbott, p. 459-60).

331 *protest:* vow solemnly.

350 *looked:* expected: Cf. *Respublica* ll. 123-4: "Oh noble Insolence, if I coulde singe as well, I wolde looke in heaven emonge Angells to dwell." (See also ll. 295, 303).

351 *good fortune . . . :* "The more knave the better lucke" (Tilley, K 130). Shift repeats the sentiment at l. 984.

scene iv

scene iv: Though the scene has no dramatic value, its appeal as sheer pageantry and its similarity to popular pageant-shows (in which Alexander, as one of the Nine Worthies, frequently figured) probably accounts for its inclusion. Such processions were a chief means of supplying the kind of spectacle that appealed to the popular audience. They appear in most of the plays produced in public theaters during the eighties. Cf. the coronation scene in *The Famous Victories*, the triumphal entries of *Tamburlaine* and *The Spanish Tragedy*, the progress of the ruler in *Friar Bacon, Three Lords and Three Ladies of London*. (Alice S. Venezky, *Pageantry on the Shakespearian Stage* [New York, 1951], pp. 20-27).

358 *Alexander*: another instance of the playwright's "classi-

cizing" of his material, since Alexander appears in
volume I of *Perceforest* but not in volumes II and III
from which he takes his plots. Alexander appears in
chapter 15 of volume I after a preliminary topograph-
ical description of Great Britain, an account of its
founding by Brutus, of the fate of Brutus' descendants
and of the extinction of his race at the death of King
Pyr, when Venus instructs the Britons to watch on the
sea-shore where they will find a king able to govern
them. At this point the romancer summarizes the action
of *Vœux du Paon*, from which *Perceforest* takes its
point of departure, describing how at the conclusion of
his Asian campaign, Alexander adopted the two sons
(Betis or Perceforest and Gadiffer) of one of his enemies, sailed with them for a temple of Venus on a
Mediterranean island and was driven by a storm to the
edge of the known world – to Great Britain – where the
inhabitants, according to Venus' oracle, are awaiting
him. After the coronation of Betis and Gadiffer as the
rulers of Britain and Scotland, Betis' vanquishment of
the enchanter Darnant and numerous episodes dependent on this action, Alexander returns to Babylon,
where he dies in the early part of the action of volume
II.

358 *as valiantly set forth as may be, and as many souldiers
as can:* an authorial direction particularly distinguished
by its permissiveness and indefiniteness. (See W. W.
Greg, *The Editorial Problem in Shakespeare* [Oxford,
1951], pp. 136-7).

365 *Pallas Temple:* Perhaps an adaptation from *Perceforest*,
which opens at the conclusion of Alexander's Asian
campaign when he sets sail for a Mediterranean island
to offer thanks for his victories at a temple of Venus.
See 358n. above.

374 *Fort of Force:* i.e. strong in its defensive works, number
of men, guns, etc.

381 *Keysar:* The *ei-ey* spelling was common during the six-

teenth century (probably as a result of Dutch or German influence). The -*ai* form – a northern form – was more common during the fourteenth and fifteenth centuries. (O.E.D.) Cf. *Apius and Virginia*, ll. 148 and 481.

400 *them print:* Bullen emends to emprint, but the reading is satisfactory as it stands.

413-14 Here and elsewhere (e.g. ll. 492-3, 972-4) the author alters the metrical pattern by inserting lines of eight iambic feet.

scene v

scene v: from *Perceforest* II, 143-144. In the romance the two knights do battle at their first meeting, but they are interrupted by the Black Knight, who admonishes them and suggests that they meet for a trial by combat fifteen days hence "au pin de la fiere merveille en la forest darrnant". The Blanc Chevalier is accompanied by a squire named Clamides whose nobility and dignity contrast strikingly with the character of Shift.

441 *princkocks:* a coxcomb, a forward youth. The etymology is obscure but the word may derive from *praecox*, hence early, precocious (O.E.D. n).

444 *such stay:* Dyce emends to such fear.

449 *denay:* deny. Cf. *Conditions*, ll. 1089, 1326, 1478; *Faerie Queene*, III, vii, 47; III, xi, 11.

451 *deprave:* deprive (O.E.D. 5).

465 *perstand:* understand. See 45n.

470 *accord to:* agree to.

474 *beray:* befoul. Cf. *Conditions*, l. 1546.

475 *Proynstone:* prune-stone.

483 *fifteenth day:* so the waiting period before the combat between the champions in *Perceforest*. The combat between the champions for the Queen of the Strange Marshes and Mustantius is to be held "the sixteene day". The customary waiting period was however 40

days. The Scottish "Order of Combats" specifies that combat is "to be performed within fourty days nixt following" after the accusation and judgement for battle; and the English ordinance dating from the reign of Richard II specifies that combat is to be *"not* within forty days" (George Neilson, *Trial by Combat* [Glasgow, 1890], p. 261).

487 *all estates:* all sorts of people.

523 *Bryan sance foy:* Dyce suggests that the name was borrowed from Spenser (*Faerie Queene*, I, ii). Since the play probably ante-dates the composition of Spenser's Book I, however, Spenser may have taken the name from *Clyomon and Clamydes* or he may have taken it independently from *Perceforest.*

535 *toy:* trick.

540 *keepe:* live.

scene vi

scenes vi-vii: Clyomon and Clamydes is "the earliest plot of English composition in which the impersonation of a lover leads to a double denouement" (i.e. recognition of Bryan's imposture and of Clamydes as the true slayer of the serpent) (Freeburg, p. 182). The motif is based on Harban's deception in II, 76 and 78. The chief alterations are the amalgamation of Harban with Bruyant, the introduction of Shift who replaces the enchantresses who aid Harban, and the reduction of the trophies to the knight's shield and the head of the flying serpent.

549 *facts:* evil, ignominious deeds. See Prologue 9n.

552 *copesmates:* rogues. Cf. Gabriel Harvey, *Pierce's Supererogation:* "The residue what soeuer, hath nothing more in it, then is vsuallie in euery ruffianly Copesmate, that hath bene a Gramer scholler, readeth riotous bokes, hanteth roisterly companie, delighteth in rude

scoffing, & karrieth a desperate minde" (ed. Grosart, 1885, II, 115-16).

560 *provoke:* invoke.

561-66 Cf. *Perceforest,* where Bruyant Sans Foy imprisons the knights of the Franc Palais in vengeance for the death of his father Darnant at the hands of Perceforest (Betis).

570 *haunt:* frequent.

570 *keep:* tend.

597 *a bucke:* i.e. a cuckold (since horned). See Partridge, p. 81.

609 *danted:* daunted.

615 *take this . . . reward:* the "chinks", money, of l. 630.

627 *jolt-headed:* thick-headed, stupid.

631 *close:* join (O.E.D. 11).

632 *ile be with him to bring:* I will accompany Clamydes.

633 *Ambodexter:* the double dealer; name of the Vice of *Cambises.*

scene vii

scene vii: an instance of the playwright's merging of two episodes and two characters. To Lyonnel du Glar's slaying of the flying serpent (II, 58) and his enchantment by Harban (II, 75-76) he adds the motif of the tournament with the Chevalier Dore and he alters Harban to Bryan, (both from III).

639 *vitall:* i.e. of life.

645 *besides:* (As) for the rest (Abbott, p. 34).

652 *Atropos:* That one of the three Fates who cuts the thread of life.

685 *prevail:* i.e. avail.

694 *cloke:* dissemble.

698b *Cary him out:* Ordinarily the stage directions maintain the theatrical point of view, designating the backstage area (i.e. the area behind the tiring house) as "in" or "within" (e.g. "Let him slip on to the Stage . . . and rise up to run in againe", "Enter after a little fight within"). The stage itself is referred to consistently as "out" (e.g. "Enter out [of the prison]"). In spite of the alteration in point of view, this stage direction, which is in the imperative, probably originated with the bookkeeper. Cf. the same direction – Carry him out – in the plot of *The Battle of Alcazar* (W. W. Greg, *Dramatic Documents from the Elizabethan Playhouses* [Oxford, 1931], I, 209).

700 *Policie:* another pseudonym for the Vice, connoting Machiavellian intrigue. (Cf. Policy, the pseudonym for Avarice, the Vice of *Respublica.*)

704 *spider catcher:* i.e. monkey.

713 *practise:* stratagem (O.E.D. 6).

713 *shell:* shield.

scene viii

scene viii: from *Perceforest* III, 5. See introduction pp. 47-49 for a discussion of the playwright's principal changes in the character of Neronis.

718-723 *"Here let them make a noyse . . . hayle out the Cockboate . . . Strike sayle, cast Ankers":* theatrical shorthand for indicating a ship in roads, a boat rowing ashore and a landing by Clyomon and the Boatswain. See Louis B. Wright, "Elizabethan Sea Drama and Its Staging", *Anglia*, LI (1927), 108. In *Perceforest* the Chevalier Dore is transported to a grove near the principal castle of the Kingdom of the Strange Marches by the spirit Zephyr.

721 *Cockboate:* small ship's boat. Cf. *Conditions*, l. 985.

722 *Shipmaister:* Q's reading – *Shiftmai.* – is apparently a compositorial confusion of *Shift* and *Shipmaister*.

725 *Enter Clyomon . . . :* presumably an addition made by the bookkeeper, necessary because the direction four lines earlier calls for action within which will suggest the

landing of a boat. The earlier direction is clearly authorial in its permissiveness ("Here let them"), its descriptiveness ("Knight of G. S.") and its indefiniteness ("with one").

729 *Ile of Strange Marshes:* i.e. foreign Marches. In *Perceforest* a lion and lioness have ravaged the land, leaving it desolate. Hence it is called the "royaulme de lestrange marche", its King explains, "pource quelle nest plus avant habitee et jen suis roy desherite & ceste dame royne evillee". (*Perceforest* II, 44.)

731 *and if:* even if (Abbott, p. 105).

732 *signed:* assigned. See 330n.

734 *Patranius:* In *Perceforest*, Neron; along with the alteration of Fergus to Thrasellus and Lyonnel to Clamydes and the addition of Mustantius, an example of the playwright's preference for classical names.

739-40 Apparently Neronis and her train enter around l. 734.

741-2 Cf. *Cambises*, ll. 861-68, beginning "Lady deer, to King a-kin, forth with let us proceed / To trace abroad the beauty fields, as erst we had decreed." The subsequent description of "blowing bud", the "sweet smel of musk white rose", the chirping birds", and "our lute and cittern" are more elaborate than is customary for the playwright of *Clyomon and Clamydes* (Dodsley IV).

752 *to trace:* i.e. walk.

761 *Fortune:* the numerous references to Fortune and the Fates are the playwright's additions. Like his alterations of the names of characters from *Perceforest*, they are apparently intended to increase the classical quality of the play.

765 *amate:* dismay, dishearten (O.E.D.).

767 *to sacke:* increase, as Dyce conjectures, "to heap – as by pouring out of a sack". Cf. l. 1257: "Hath sackt on me such hugie heapes of seaceles sorrowes here". The word is not listed in the O.E.D.

776 *fame:* rumor.

779 *Combat wise:* i.e. dressed for combat.

scene ix

830 *prepare:* repair.

835 *pretence:* intention.

840 "Faint-hearted knaves never win fair women" (Tilley,
    H 302). Cf. *Conditions*, l. 1499: "Experience showes
    faint harted knights wins neuer fayre ladies loue"; also
    Fidele and Fortunio, l. 419; *Faerie Queene*, IV, x, 53.

scene x

scene x: At this point the playwright combines the deception of
    Harban with the enmity of Bruyant Sans Foy for the
    knights of the Franc Palais, which belongs to a later
    episode. During the waiting period that the Fairy Queen
    imposes on Lyonnel, he falls in the snares of an enchant-
    ress, who brings about his imprisonment in Bruyant's
    castle, where he finds other knights of the realm. The
    prisoners are rescued by the knights of the Franc Palais,
    not by Lyonnel (III, 12-13). Clamydes lament (ll. 872-
    895) has its counterpart in Lyonnel's lay of complaint
    II, 77) when he has been deceived by Harban.

853 *in:* unstressed Elizabethan pronunciation of "e'en".

863 *imploy:* intend. A form of imply (O.E.D. 2, e).

872 *Clamydes in prison:* The scene is staged with Clamydes
    speaking either from an upper station or from behind a
    grate. Shift advises him to "Looke out at the windowe";
    he says that he will "open the prison doores" and when
    he does so, he says "so the doores are open" and the
    accompanying stage direction reads *"Enter out"*. Com-
    pare the staging of the prison scene in *Two Noble
    Kinsmen* where at least one of the prisoners in II. i. is
    "above": the first direction reads "Enter Palamon, and
    Arcite, above"; the jailer says "that's *Arcite* looks out"
    but he is corrected when his daughter answers "No sir,
    no, that's *Palamon: Arcite* is the lower of the twaine;
    you may perceive a part of him".

873 *Tyre:* Dyce and Bullen emend to *Tire of,* but since *Tyre* was frequently pronounced as a disyllable – like other monosyllables ending in *-r* or *-re* – the line is regular metrically as it stands (Abbott, p. 480).

881 *pind:* imprisoned.

894 *amates:* dismays, disheartens. Cf. l. 765.

917 *sentence:* a formal opinion in answer to a solemn question; hence Shift's mockery.

934 *condition:* social rank, or more probable, moral nature.

942 *joy that is my joy:* enjoy what (i.e. Juliana) is my joy.

967 *Enter Shift, with a bag . . . of gold:* "The English dramatists were especially fond of depicting a clown who has suddenly come into a great fortune and struts about ridiculously bedizened in gorgeous apparel and haughtily patronises his companions. Even in so early a work as *Clyomon and Clamydes . . .* we are confronted with a clown thus suddenly enriched. And though I know of no other instance taken from an early play which might be cited, it is nevertheless highly probable that we have here one of those very ancient farcial *motifs* whose popularity we are unable to trace through the centuries owing to the absence of records. . . ." Wilhelm Creizenach, *The English Drama in the Age of Shakespeare* (London, 1916, p. 297.

986 *passeth:* surpasses (though here intransitive).

988 *over-go:* leave (me) behind (O.E.D. 10).

scene xi

scene xi: From *Perceforest* II, 5, though the playwright's alterations in the love scene are extensive (see introduction, pp. 43, 47-49).

992-1001 *How Can that tree:* a paraphrase of "No pleasure without som pain", no. 71 in *The Paradise of Dainty Devices,* assigned to Lord Vaux in all but one of the nine editions (the undated edition of 1596). It appeared also in

William Barley's *New Book of Tablature* (1596) and in a song book of 1626. (See William Chappell's *Old English Popular Music*, I, 72). Cf. also *Richard III*. II. ii. 41-42. The poem is printed in full in Appendix C.

1012 *force no crueltie:* single out, exaggerate; hence putting a cruel interpretation on his actions.

1007 *vades:* fade, chiefly figurative. Cf l. 1087.

1017 *gesters:* gestures, deportment, bearing. The spelling is the obsolete form for the verb, not the noun.

1019 *allegate:* allege.

1052 *absolve:* solve.

1053 *propound:* proposition, possibly riddle. The only example of this obsolete noun in the O.E.D.

1055 Neronis' confession of her affection for Clyomon before any advances on his part is an early example of a motif that was to become increasingly popular in English comedy. Cf. *Conditions*, ll. 857-871, *The Arraignment of Paris*, II. ii, *Dido, Queen of Carthage*, III. iv. For other examples see Forsythe, p 65

1066 *brought in former rate:* restored to her former condition or value.

1075 *if case:* if it should happen that.

1076 *seeme:* attempt, think fit.

1080 *define:* explain.

1082 *to moove:* to ask (O.E.D. 14, 6).

1104 *in gage:* as security.

1105 *prevail:* avail.

1105 *Jewell:* In *Perceforest*, Nerones gives the Chevalier Dore a ring which enables her to recognize him in a subsequent scene when she is disguised as a shepherd and he as a pilgrim. The playwright makes no dramatic use of the jewell, but he may have suggested the use of the rings in *Two Gentlemen* (see Freeburg, p. 70).

1114 *grudge:* complain.

1119 *in way of right:* justly.

scene xii

scene xii: From *Perceforest* III, 33, where the Norwegian King
        Fergus attempts to win Nerones' hand by undertaking
        the defense of an island for one month. It is the custom
        in the Kingdom of the Strange Marches that whoever
        would win the princess' hand must guard "lisle de les-
        preuve qui est soubz ceste place [Neron's castle] au
        meillieu de la riviere et quel soit la soixante jours",
        defending it against all other knights who come to lay
        claim to the lady's hand. The playwright substitutes a
        disguise-plot and has the kidnapping of Neronis be the
        Norwegian King's prime motive.
1138 *your aydes be prest with mine:* your men be impressed
        with mine.
1159 *ure:* use.

scene xiii

scene xiii: From *Perceforest* III, 34, where the Chevalier Dore,
        after numerous adventures of which the chief is his en-
        counter with the "beste glatissant", learns about the
        treachery of the King of Norway from a dream, a
        maiden whom Nerones has sent to him, and from an
        old woman who lives near Neron's castle. The play-
        wright replaces all three with Rumor.
1167 *castle of comfort:* Tilley, C 121; also the title of one of
        Thomas Becon's works.
1196 *Rumor:* Cf. *Apius and Virginia,* l. 861 and *Grissell,* sig.
        G3v. The traditional images for depicting Rumor (or
        Fame) – wings, tongues, lips, eyes – are traceable ulti-
        mately to the *Æneid* IV, 180-195. Though no indication
        of costume is given here, mere introduction of Rumor
        probably involved a costume that would make graphic
        his qualities. For example, Holinshed, describing a
        pageant at the court of Henry VIII, tells how there "en-

tered a person called Report, apparelled in crimson satin, full of toongs or chronicles". In *2 Henry IV*, Rumor enters "painted full of tongues". Dekker's "The Magnificent Entertainment", 11. 752-56, gives directions for Fame: "A Woman in a Watchet Roabe, thickly set with open Eyes, and Tongues, a payre of large golden Winges at her backe, a Trumpet in her hand, a Mantle of sundry cullours trauersing her body: all these Ensignes desplaying but the propertie of her swiftnesse, and aptnesse to disperse Rumours" (ed. Fredson Bowers, 1955). Campion's "Masque written for the Earl of Somerset's Marriage" (1614) introduces "Rumor in a skin coate full of winged Tongues, and over it an antic robe; on his head a Cap like a tongue, with a large pair of wings to it" (ed. Percival Vivian, 1909). Cf. also Chaucer, *The House of Fame* III, 11. 1360-1418 (ed. Robinson, 1957).

1205 *Mustantius:* In *Perceforest*, the dispute over the crown takes place in the land of Borras. The playwright transfers the dispute to the Ile of Strange Marshes as a means of welding the three episodes together. He further provides that Alexander be the peace-maker in the dispute whereas in *Perceforest*, Alexander returns to Macedon in volume I and dies there at the beginning of volume II.

1210 *pretend:* intend.

1219 *what:* why (Abbott, p. 253).

scene xiv

1243 *martris:* like "languishes" (l. 143), one of Shift's malapropisms; his meaning is "martyr".

scene xv

scene xv: The account of Neronis' disguise comes from *Perceforest* III, 35 which comes, in turn, from Gerbert de Montreuil's *Roman de la Violette*. (Lods, pp. 76-77.)

Actually Neronis assumes two disguises – the garb of a page here and in sc. xx and of a "Sheepheards boy" in sc. xviii. Though the disguised heroine had been a conventional feature of Italian *commedia erudita* since the 1530's, *Clyomon and Clamydes* and *The Wars of Cyrus* (c. 1576-77) are among the earliest English plays to adopt the motif. Its subsequent popularity is of course well attested. It appears in the eighties, for example, in *Gallathea* (1584-5), *Soliman and Perseda* (1585) and *The Scottish History of James the Fourth*. The mistaken wooing of Neronis by another woman (ll. 1395-1410), her sentimental farewell (ll. 1570-71), her apology for wearing a men's clothing (ll. 1261-1264), her expression of weariness from travel (ll. 1513-1514) all become part of the dramatic tradition of the disguised heroine (see Freeburg, p. 63).

1254   *in the Forrest:* the only indication in a stage direction of scene-location, it is very likely authorial. On the subject of the stage forest see introduction pp. 34-35.

1281-84   In *Perceforest* III, 35, Nerones feigns death, escapes from her coffin at night, makes her way to a farmhouse and there, at the suggestion of an old peasant woman, assumes the disguise of a shepherd boy.

1287   On Corin see introduction, p. 45.

1290   *conswade:* The only example of this dialectical word given, in the O.E.D.

1298   *let them laugh that win:* "He laughs that wins" (Tilley L93). Cf. *Patient Grissell,* l. 957; *Promos and Cassandra,* II, i.

1299   *vorty pence:* The usual amount for a small bet, as in Greene's *The Art of Coneycatching:* "Wager's Laying, & – forty pence gaged against a match of wrestling"; also the usual amount for an attorney's fee (e.g. *All's Well,* II. ii. 22). When money was reckoned by pounds, marks, and nobles, forty pence was half of a noble – hence the proverb "Farewell, forty pence, Jack Noble is dead" (Tilley, F 618).

1300 *lookes:* expects.

1304 *cursen:* Christian.

1304 *averd:* afeared.

1308 *courtnold:* contemptuous name for a courtier. Cf. *Respublica,* l. 1585: "hither cam a zorte of courtnalls, harde men & zore".

1310 *they leest:* thee liest; an instance of the levelling of singular *thou, thee* and plural *ye, you* to *thee, we, ye,* (see Westlake, "People's Dialect, Part II", *Respublica,* p. 75).

1311 *crackropes:* a rogue, one who is headed for the gallows. Cf. *Apius and Virginia,* l. 254: "You codshed you crackerope, you chattering pye"; and *Damon and Pithias,* l. 1344: "Away you cracke ropes, are you fighting at the court gate?"

1319 *Whow:* how.

1327 *set leekes:* The meaning is not clear. To eat the leek means to submit to humiliation under compulsion (O. E.D. 4, b), but the lines seems to refer to the "clap" mentioned at l. 1298.

1328 *canvosing:* from tossing in a sheet or blanket and hence, to make love (Partridge, pp. 74 and 84).

1329 *bonnomablely:* Cf. People's distortions of words in *Respublica* – e.g. ll. 655-656: "*Respub.* It passeth anie mans Imaginacion. / *people.* youe zai zouth; yt passeth anie mans madge mason".

1335 *like man:* "As the man is so is his talk" (Tilley, M 75).

scene xvi

scene xvi: from *Perceforest* III, 34. Corin replaces the hermit – the "ancien preudhomme", once a rich man and a "bachelor" – who finds the Chevalier Dore and nurses him back to health.

1339 *glozd:* flattered.

1389 *foltring:* faltring. The O.E.D. notes that ME. *falden* (fold) was used to describe the limbs or tongue. *Falter,* it says, may be the result of the formation of *falden* with roughly synonymous verbs like *balter, totter, welter.* See *Lucrece,* 1768.

1385 *gorde:* soaked, covered.

1391 *his dog:* On the use of trained animals on the stage, see Louis B. Wright, "Animal Actors on the English Stage Before 1642", *PMLA,* XLII (1927), 656-669; W. J. Lawrence, *Those Nut-Cracking Elizabethans* (London, 1935), pp. 9-27.

1393 *like a stocke:* stock-fish (dried cod). Tilley (S 867) cites Thomas Becon's Catechism VI, p. 355: "Those parents . . . which furiously rage against their children, and beat them as stockfish".

1397 *whorcop:* horcop, bastard. Cf. *Respublica,* ll. 679-80: "There is vorste and vormooste Flatterie, ill a bee, / A slypper, suger-mowthed howrecoop as can be". Also ll. 698, 716, 1593.

1400 *controms:* controller (of accounts) – the only example of this word given in the O.E.D.

1413 *whither:* Q reads whather, a doubtful form (Eduard Eckhardt, *Die Dialekttypen* [Louvain, 1910] pp. 28-29).

1417 *vorty pence:* See 1299n.

1428 *surringer:* apparently a malapropism for surgeon.

1439 *herse:* coffin.

1444 A word may have been omitted from the end of the line, though it is metrically complete. Dyce adds "plain".

1444-48 The details are from *Perceforest* III, 34.

1447 *passengers:* passers-by.

1449 *with a Hearse:* Cf. *The Arraignment of Paris,* l. 771: "The shepherds bring in Collins Hearce singing". Also *Richard III* (Q 1597), II i: "Enter Lady Anne with the hearse of Harry the 6".

1456 *a life:* on my life. Cf *Winters Tale,* IV. iv. 264.

scene xvii

scene xvii: The coffin, shields and swords remain on stage during
this scene.

1477-78 *very brave:* finely dressed. The phrase appears often in
stage directions. Eg. *Thomas of Woodstock*, 1. 350:
"Enter Woodstock very braue ..."; *Taming of the
Shrew* (F), 1. 219: "Enter Tranio braue. ..." Shift's
gown is probably comparable to Haphazard's in *Apius
and Virginia*, ll. 207-210: "Yet a proper Gentileman I
am of truthe / Yea that may yee see by my long side
gowne, / Yea but what am I, a Scholer, or a schole-
maister, or els some youth. A Lawier, a studient. ..."

scene xviii

scene xviii: from *Perceforest* III, 38, where Nerones likewise mistakes Fergus' tomb for her lover's but learns of her
error when she finds the Chevalier Dore's armour in a
woodland temple to Venus (where the hermit directed
him to leave it) and not, as in the play, when she reads
the verses handed to her by Providence.

1515 *simple ... feete:* Apparently a memorial error on the
part of the compositor.

1518 *hand ... showe:* Neronis has a shepherd's hook in her
hand.

1523 *rate:* rank, condition (O.E.D. III, 9).

1526 *distilled drops, for to bedew:* Dyce suggests, but does not
adopt, the emendation though "distill my face" is obviously erroneous. The appearance of "distilling teares"
at l. 1524 strengthens the case for the emendation.

1532 With Neronis' discovery of what she believes to be her
lover's body and her attempted suicide, compare *Cymbeline* IV. ii. 291-332 (see Freeburg, p. 64n).

1541 *Lachis:* the Fate who spins the thread of events.

1549 *Descend:* On the special significance of the staging, see introduction, pp. 31-33. Compare the virtue in the morality play who appears in time to save the sinner from suicide; here the difference is significant. Despair affects the heroine not because of her sins but because of the loss of her lover.

1552 *prepaire:* repair.

1558 *to tender:* to pity, have mercy on.

scene xix

scene xix: Clyomon's decision to champion the cause of Neronis' mother against Mustantius is a device for condensing and unifying the episodes from the romance. Before the Chevalier Dore and the disguised Nerones arrive in the land of Borras, they meet at the castle of Pernehan, where the Chevalier Dore vanquishes the giant Branq and receives the squire Cueur Dacier as a gift from his grateful host. Together the two lovers travel into Scotland, but it is only when the Chevalier Dore reassumes his original armour that Nerones begins to suspect that he is her lover. Cf. scene xx.

scene xx

1623 *strangely disguised:* i.e. like a foreigner.

1639 *Cur Daceer:* In *Perceforest*, Nerones receives the name from the woman with whom she takes refuge after her escape from Fergus (III, 35).

scene xxi

1658 *Somnus:* god of sleep.

1659 *shrowd the day:* i.e. hide [during] the day.

1661 Since Clamydes' ten-day enchantment, at least sixteen

more days have elapsed. Hence Bryan's fear of day-
time travel is a necessary addition to explain his delay
in arriving at the court of Denmark.

1673 *force:* care, regard. Cf. *Conditions,* ll. 1360, 1504, 1634;
Apius and Virginia, l. 674.

1674 *whereas*: where.

scene xxii

scene xxii: From *Perceforest* III, 40, though greatly altered. Arriving in the "royaulme de Borre" where a dispute has
arisen over the succession to the throne, the Chevalier
Dore offers his services in combat to one of the claimants
and, entering the lists, finds himself confronted by his
old enemy the Blanc Chevalier. The fierceness of their
combat prompts the disputing nobles of Borras to settle
their dispute peaceably and so to save the lives of two
such valiant knights. The knights, however, continue to
fight until Coeur Dacier approaches the four famous
knights – Troylus, Lyonnel, Estonne and Gadiffer – who
number among the spectators and berates them for al-
lowing the slaughter that will inevitably ensue unless
they put a stop to the combat. The knights are thor-
oughly abashed and they approach the combatants to
persuade them to settle their dispute peacefully. The
Blanc Chevalier agrees on the condition that he learn
the Chevalier Dore's name, but the Chevalier Dore refuses until the matter is brought to a happy issue when
Gadiffer, his brother, recognizes him.

1676 *Wiffler:* Whiffler, one whose duty it was to clear the
way for processions. Equipped with swords, the whifflers' duty was to keep people from coming too near
the procession or interfering with it. The whifflers'
uniform probably varied from city to city, but it was
apparently of a grandeur consistent with important
civic occasions. An account of a muster of the citizens

of London during the reign of Henry VIII describes the whifflers on horseback as garbed "all yn cotes of white damaske over theyre harnes, mounted on good horrses well trappyd, with great chaynes aboute theyre necks, and propre javelyns or battle axes yn theyre handes, with cappes of velvett on theyre heddes with ryche ouches" and those on foot as men "apparellyd yn whyte sylke or buffe jerkyns, without harnes, with whyte hose and whyte shoes, every man having a slaugh sworde or javelyn to kepe the people yn araye, with chaynes aboute their neckes, and fethers in theyre cappes". "The Meaning of the Word 'Whiffler'," in *The Gentleman's Magazine*, Vol. 121, n.s. Vol. 37 (Feb. 1852), p. 155. See also Robert Withington, *English Pageantry* (Cambridge, Harvard University Press, 1918), I, 71.

1709 *an:* one (Abbott, p. 79).

1726 *conge:* congey or congee. Usually a ceremonial farewell or leavetaking. Here, by extension, it appears to mean leave, permission. Hence, there by full permission to the challenger there (where he) stands.

1727 *of sufferance commeth ease:* Tilley, S 955. See also no. 37, *The Paradise of Dainty Devices.*

1733 *three houres space:* Cf. the Scottish "The Order of Combats": ". . . in cace the Defender did not come at the tym convenient, in the day appoynted, then did the King delyver his pleasur to the Constable, and he reported the same unto the Marishall, who ffurthwith did give order unto the lieutenant that the Defender should presently be called to appear, by the Herauld Marischall, after this maner: *OIEZ!* G.D., Defendant in this combat! Appear now! ffor in this day thou hast taken upon thee to acquitt thy pledges in presence of the Lord Constable and Marishall; And also defend thy person against A.B., who challenged thee to mentaine this combat. This proclamation was made thryce at the end of the lists. But if, at the second tym, the partie appeared not, then the Herauld did add these

words: The day passeth and therfore come without
delay! And if in cace the said Defendant appeared not
befor noon, but stayed untill the third hour after, then
did the Herauld, by comandment of the Constable, in
the beginning of the proclamation say: A.B. appear in
haist, and save thy honour! ffor the day is weill near
spent wherein thow did promise to perform thy enter-
pryse!" George Neilson, *Trial by Combat* (Glasgow,
1890), pp. 264-265. Cf. *Lear*, V. iii. 115-117.

1774 On the stock incident of the formal combat and recon-
ciliation of the combatants, compare *Jocasta* IV. i. v.
2; *2 Henry VI*, II. 3; *Richard II*, I. 3; *Troilus and
Cresseida*, IV. 5. (For others, see Forsythe, p. 309.)

1788 *discharge:* charge.

1796-7 *sier/desier:* Still another "auricular figure" recommen-
ded by Puttenham as a way a poet may "alter his
wordes ... for pleasure to giue a better sound, sometimes vpon necessitie, and to make vp the rime". He
cites both *sier* and *desier* as alteration by the displace-
ment of syllables (Puttenham, p. 174).

1839 In *Perceforest*, the discovery is effected by a slash in the
Chevalier Dore's (Clyomon's) clothing which reveals a
distinguishing birthmark.

scene xxiii

scene xxiii: The three episodes from *Perceforest* come together
in the final scene. Harban's deception of the Fairy
Queen, Perceforest and Blanche belongs to II, 78-79
and the penetration of his disguise by the Fairy Queen
to II, 80. The reunion of Lyonnel and Blanche belongs
to the beginning of IV. The penetration of Nerones'
disguise by the Fairy Queen and her reunion with the
Chevalier Dore belongs to III, 42. Neither the Queen
of Denmark nor Juliana retains the powers of magic
of the Fairy Queen and Blanche whom they replace.
In *Perceforest* the "Dames de la Foret" who have learn-

ed magic in order to defend themselves against Darnant, teach their science to Queen Lydoire, whom they dub the Fairy Queen and she, in turn, bequeaths her knowledge to her daughter.

1898 *sup:* taste.

1940 *of truth the which:* possibly "the truth of which" is the proper reading.

1958 Knowledge has not been in Clyomon's service since scene iii.

1988 Cf. *Grissel,* ll. 986-988: "A Dido for her Chastitie, Penellope for truth, / A Thisbe for her ardent love, and Pyramus insueth: / Cassandra shee for pacyence, full aptly maye be namde."

1991 *sad:* sober, serious.

2009 *bound:* boon.

2044 A line is presumably missing which would complete the couplet.

2058 The meeting of a character with his imposter was later to become a stock incident. See Forsythe, p. 245, for examples.

2064 *too:* to.

2075-6 A line is presumably missing which would complete the couplet.

2079 *name so much:* great name (Abbott, p. 51).

2084 *not for the eares of my head:* Tilley, E 15.

2116 Apparently the end of the line has been dropped.

2131-35 *pageant ... motions ... motion:* conceivably an allusion to *periaktoi.* See William E. Miller, "Periaktoi in the Old Blackfriars", *MLN,* LXXIV (1959), 1-3 and "Periaktoi: Around Again", *SQ,* XV (1964), 61-65.

2133 The Vice's function as interpreter of the action for the audience is extended so that he comes to be thought of as the mover of the action, the presenter of the play. Cf. *Martins Months Mind* (1589): "Roscius pleades in the Senate house; Asses play upon harpes; the Stage is brought into the Church; and vices make plaies of Church matters. . . ." (Chambers III, 230).

2138 *scacely:* scarcely, only just now.

2148ff. From here to the end of the play the fourteener gives way to eight-foot iambic couplets, an alteration that presumably reflects the unrevised portion of the author's papers. See introduction pp. 17-18.

2156 *if gods to fore:* if the gods assist or favor. Cf. *Cornelia*, II. 268: "Else, God tofore, myself may live to see / His tired corse lie toiling in his blood". (Dodsley) Cf. the similar construction *God before* in *Henry V*, I. ii. 307-8; III. vi. 164-5.

2160 *glistering:* glittering.

2171 *Say on your mind:* The line, printed in italics in Q, is given to Neronis. Apparently a marginal insertion, it interrupts the couplet and may be a note directing the actor to extemporize. But cf. *Damon and Pithias*, 1. 1155, where the same words make a part of the dialogue: "Then say on thy mind."

2184 *who gave you drink:* A significant inconsistency here and at l. 2194. Clyomon meets Neronis in scene xx where she has entered "like the Page", but he does not meet her in shepherd's garb. Neither does he receive refreshment from her (in shepherd's garb) after he has slain the King of Norway. On the significance of the reference for the text see introduction p. 18.

APPENDIX A

EMENDATIONS OF ACCIDENTALS

Prologue

7 aspire,] ~:

scene i

5 rate:] ~.
51 take.] ~,
55 consent.] ~,
58 yours   ] ~,
68 heart] *r* broken in most copies
70 same:] ~.
77 Knight:] ~,

scene ii

116 breake:] ~,
126 bootes?] ~,
135 Knowledge] knowledge
138 Knowledge] knowledge
139 Knowledge] knowledge
149 Knowledge] knowledge
166 Knowledge] knowledge
166 stay,] ~:
167 play:] ~,
178 ring,] corrected in B, P, W

187 game,] ∼.
191 knowen,] ∼.
191 Knight] Kight
199 Knowledge] knowledge
202 Knowledge] knowledge
206 togither] to-gither (turnover)
211 Knowledge] knowledge

scene iii

220 *King] Ring*
231 therefore,] comma faint in some copies
238 Widow,] ∼
245 trace,] ∼.
254 shame:] colon blurred in most copies
265 Knowledge] knowledge
298 carc,] ∼:
299 name:] ∼,
308 find,] ∼.
313 undertake:] *a* blurred in most copies
317 atchived,| ∼:
318 deprived:] ∼.
327 Knowledge] knowledge
329 Knowledge] knowledge
338 Knowledge] knowledge
342 sort] *r* broken in most copies
344 Knowledge] knowledge
346 *Exit.] (Exit.*
349 before] bfore
357 *Exit.] (Exit.*

scene iv

363 toile.] ∼,
364 *Mars* I] *Mars*I
376 hold?] ∼,
377 doubt:] ∼?

381 Keysar] *Keysar*
381 ground?] ~,
388 thee:] ~,
389 see,] ~:
398 man:] ~,
409 *Pallas*] Pallas

scene v

421 thing:] ~.
433 toyle:] ~,
439 Knowledge] knowledge
442 hall,] ~.
446 Knowledge] knowledge
473 Knowledge] knowledge
491 strengths:] ~,
516 fifteene] fifteeene
522 Knowledge] knowledge
523 there?] ~
524 Knowledge] knowledge
529 Knowledge] knowledge
541 to bring] tobring
542 them:] ~,
547 *Exit.*] ~:

scene vi

564 try,] ~.
569 *Denmarks*] Denmarks
580 away,] ~:
581 Knight:] ~,
601 Knowledge] knowledge
624 *Exit.*] *Exeunt.*
627 jolt-headed] jolt headed in P
633 Ambodexter] ambodexter

scene vii

643 Knight,] ~.
644 heere.] ~,
645 beare,] ~:
662 *and*] and
667 all] second *l* faint in most copies
672 apparell:] ~,
674 Knowledge] knowledge
676 make:] ~,
700 Policie] policie
706 shalt] *lt* blurred in all copies except B

scene viii

725 Clyomon] Clyomomon
725 *Boateswaine*] *Boate swaine*
727 *Boateswaine.*] *Boatswaine.*
736 Boateswaine] *Boateswaine*
746 wonne.] corrected in B and F
761 Fortune] *Fortune*
763 blind,] ~.
764 be.] ~,
769 day,] ~.
770 there,] ~:
777 disgraced,] defaced:
781 releefe] *r* broken in J
784 not,] ~
804 small] fmall
808 travell] type loose in some copies
819 *Jove*] Jove

scene ix

825 on,] ~
834 Knowledge] knowledge

scene x

864 sake:] ∼,
886 Fortune] fortune
891 Dame Honours] dame honours
898 againe.] ∼,
920 is:] ∼,
921 amis,] ∼:
928 Knowledge] knowledge
939b *Exit.*] *Exeunt.*
940 *Clamydes,*] ∼
947 *l. Knight*] 1 Knight
955 depart:] ∼,
956 hart,] ∼:
962 Knowledge] knowledge
972 Knowledge] knowledge
974 certaintie,] ∼.
984 plaine.] ∼,

scene xi

1037 allow:] ∼,
1057 depraves,] ∼:
1060 furious] *r* broken in all copies
1064 sound:] ∼
1068 might – – –] ∼.
1095 deare] deate
1112 Fortune] *Fortune*

scene xii

1125 case,] ∼:
1128 force] *r* broken in two copies
1130 sway,] ∼:
1142 *1. Lord*] *1 Lord*
1156 *2. Lord*] *2 Lord*
1161 *1. Lord*] *1 Lord*

scene xiii

1187 supprest,] ∼.
1188 ought:] ∼,
1201 *Norway*] Norway
1204 behind,] ∼.
1212 *Norway*] Norway
1214 provide:] ∼.
1216 *Norway*] Norway
1217 Fortune] fortune

scene xiv

1226 Knowledge] knowledge
1236 *Denmarke*] Denmarke
1246 and] And
1246 foote,] ∼:
1248 come] came
1254 mans apparell] hyphen added in **H**

scene xv

1267 *Norway*] Norway
1279 *Norway*] Norway
1298 you, my nabor] you my nabor,
1304 averd] a verd
1313 be.] ∼
1314 me,] ∼
1320 *Madge*] Madge
1327 sacke] scake

scene xvi

1360 stroke:] colon cut off in most copies
1374 assaile.] ∼,
1377 receive.] ∼,
1391 Corin] Coryn

1392 a ha] A ha
1407 it:] ∼,
1408 it,] ∼
1415 *Corin.*] *Coryn.*
1420 *Corin.*] *Coryn.*
1427 *Corin.*] *Coryn.*
1426 *Corin.*] *Coryn.*
1438 aright,] ∼:
1441 *Corin.*] *Coryn.*
1449 Corin] Coryn
1463 *Corin.*] *Coryn.*

scene xvii

1485 famed,] ∼
1491 is,] ∼.
1504 land,] ∼:

scene xviii

1515 feete   ] ∼,
1517 Fortune] *Fortune*
1553 *Jove*] Jove
1562 *Jove*] Jove
1566 praise,] corrected in F

scene xx

1608 griesly] griefly
1615 *Norway*] Norway
1616 bee,] ∼:
1635 strange] may be ftrange in H and J
1640 boy,] ∼:

scene xxii

1704 glad,] ∼

1791 vow] ~:
1793 Grace] Gtace
1794 strife,] strifes
1794 sir Knights] ~,
1805 frame] ~,
1806 him:] ~,
1812 bear,] ~
1813 here   ] ~?
1814 daughter,] ~
1814 *Norway*] Norway
1815 bring,] ~.
1820 *Norway*] Norway
1823 have.] ~
1841 unknowne.] knowne,
1856 *Jove*] Jove
1865 returne.] ~,
1872 Fortune] fortune
1876 Fortune] fortune

scene xxiii

1913 embrace   ] ~.
1921 hest] heft in B and P (?)
1934 ay.] ~,
1942 *King.*] *Kiag.*
1949 refuse,] ~.
1970 Fortune] fortune
1972 Fortune] fortune
1980 Fortune] fortune
1984 Fortune] fortune
1995 be:] ~,
1997 Fortune] fortune
2010 found:] ~,
2017 King,] ~.
2018 for my] formy
2019 what] whad
2026 pretend.] ~,

2039 great,] ∼
2051 no sister you] no siste you; in some copies, no sistey ou
2057 *Clamydes*] ∼,
2057 be,] ∼
2063 *Clyomon.*] *Clio.*
2096 cowardly] cowarly
2133 Knowledge]*Knowledge*
2142 Knowledge] *Knowledge*
2156 fore,] ∼
2159 he's] he'is
2162 *Neronis.*] Nerones.
2170 crave.] ∼,
2171 Say on your mind.] *Say on your mind.*
2171-2 One line in Q.
2207 Fortune] *Fortune*

Addenda:

436 Adieu] Adiu
614 beast.] ∼
765 Fortune] *Fortune*
818 Fortune] *Fortune*
1508 come] came
1552 *Providence*] Providence
1708 I] ∼,
1718 day.] ∼?

APPENDIX B

THE ROMANTIC PLAY 1570-1585

Principal evidence of the vogue of the romantic play during the period 1570-1585 is to be found in the accounts of the Revels Office, which preserve the titles of some 63 plays [1] – most of them lost – that were presented at court during those years. Of these, at least 23 [2] are usually classified – on the basis of their titles – as romantic plays. Aside from the court records, evidence is meager. Contemporary literature and records give the titles of an additional 51 lost plays which were produced during the same period,[3] but of these, only four may be classified as romances: *Delphrigius King of Fairies* (c. 1570),[4] *The Red Knight* (1576), *The Blacksmith's Daughter* (1578), and *The Queen of Ethiopia* (1578).[5]

[1] Charles William Wallace, *The Evolution of the English Stage up to Shakespeare* (Berlin, 1912), pp. 203-209. Chambers and James Paul Brawner count 65 plays for the same period. (See Chambers, III, 178; James Paul Brawner, *The Wars of Cyrus* [Urbana, Illinois, 1942], pp. 64-66.)

[2] The classification is taken from Alfred Harbage, *Annals of English Drama 975-1700, op. cit.*, pp. 40-51. "The historie of the Rape of the second Helene," for which Ellison finds a source indicating that it was also a romantic play, and *The Rare Triumphs of Love and Fortune*, which Harbage classifies as a mythological moral play, are added to Harbage's list. (See Ellison, *op. cit.*, pp. 64-66.) For similar classifications of the court plays see Chambers, II, 178, n2; Brawner, *op. cit.*, pp. 64-66.

[3] Harbage lists 48 lost plays for 1570-85. (*Annals, op cit.*, pp. 40-51.) To these may be added three others: *Hemidos and Thelay* (1570), *Holofernes* (1576) and *Julius Caesar* (1582). (See Gertrude Marian Sibley, *The Lost Plays and Masques 1500-1642* [Ithaca, New York, 1933].)

[4] Harbage lists this as one play. Sibley considers it as two.

[5] For allusions and records containing these titles see Sibley and Chambers, IV, 398-404 *passim*.

Among the 24 plays which were printed during those years only one – *Common Conditions* – belongs to the type. (*The Rare Triumphs of Love and Fortune* was not printed until 1589 and *Clyomon and Clamydes* did not reach print until 1599.) Yet thirty titles representing 27 lost plays and three extant plays remain to indicate the popularity of the romantic play during the generation of the 1570's and 1580's. Even the paucity of evidence outside the court hardly serves to remove the impression of a vigorous romantic drama that competed for popularity with the late morality and with the nascent classical and realistic drama both in and out of Court.

The following is a list of the thirty romantic plays produced between the years 1570 and 1585, indicating their dates of performance, the names of the acting companies, and the conjectured sources. Unless otherwise specified, material on the sources is from Ellison, *The Early Romantic Drama at the English Court*. The titles of the lost court plays are starred.

1570

Delphrigius King of Fairies
> Known only from allusions in Nashe's "To the Gentlemen Students of Both Universities" and in Greene's "Groats-worth of Wit".

1571

Dec. 27 *Lady Barbara* * – *Lane's*

1572

Dec. 25 *The play of Cariclia* * – Leicester's
> Heliodorus, *Æthiopian History*, Book X.

Feb. 17 *Cloridon and Radiamanta* * – Lane's
> *Orlando Furioso*, canto 37.

Feb. 19 *Paris and Vienna* * – Westminster
> "History of the noble and ryght valyant and worthy Knyght Parys and the fayr Vyene the daulphyns doughter of Vynnois", pub. Caxton, 1485.

1573

Dec. 26 *Predor and Lucia* * – Leicester's
Dec. 28 *Mamillia* * – Leicester's

1574

Jan. 3 *Herpetulus the blew knighte & perobia* * – Clinton's
Feb. 2 *Timoclia at the sege of Thebes by Alexander* * – Merchant
Taylors
Feb. 21 *Philemon & philecia* * – Leicester's
Dec. 14 *Phedrastus* * – Chamberlain's
Phigon and Lucia * – (rehearsed)
Dec. 27 *Pretestus* * – Clinton's

1575

Jan. 1 *Panecia* * – Leicester's
> Bandello 1. (22?). Versions of the same tale are found also in
> Belleforest's *Histoires Tragiques* and in *Orlando Furioso*, V.

1576

Common Conditions
Dec. 26 *The Paynter's Daughter* * – Warwick's
July 29-Aug. 5 *The Red Knight* – Chamberlain's at Bristol

1577

Feb. 17 *The Historie of the Solitarie Knight* * – Howard's
> "The pretie History of Arnalt and Lucinda" trans. Claudius Holy-
> band; derives ultimately from "Le Chevalier Melancholique" (?) or
> from ch. 84-95 of the twelfth book of the French *Amadis*.
Feb. 18 *The Irisshe Knyght* * – Warwick's
> exploits of Morhoult of Ireland from Arthurian romance.

1578

The Blacksmith's Daughter
> Known only by allusion in Gosson, "The School of Abuse".[6]

6 Quoted in Chambers, IV, 204.

Aug. 31-Sept. 6 *The Queen of Ethiopia* – Howard's at Bristol

Heliodorus, *Æthiopian History* (?).

Jan. 6 *The Historie of the Rape of the Second Helene* * – Chamberlain's

Part I, *Florisel de Niquea.*

1579

Mar. 1 *The history of the Knight in the Burnyng Rock* * – Warwick's

Margaret Tyler's *The First part of the Mirrour of Princely Deeds and Knighthood.*

Dec. 26 *A history of the Duke of Millayn and the Marques of Mantua* * – Chamberlain's

1580

Feb. 2 *The history of Portio and demorantes* * – Chamberlain's

Feb. 14 *The historye of the Soldan and the Duke of* – Derby's

1582

Dec. 30 *The Rare Triumphs of Love and Fortune* – Derby's

1583

Clyomon and Clamydes – Queen's

Perceforest, vols. II and III.

Feb. 12 *A historie of Ariodante and Geneuora* * – Merchant Taylors

Orlando Furioso, V; or Peter Beverly's translation (1566) [7]

1585

Jan. 3 *The history of felix &philiomena* * – Queen's

Montemayor's *Diana.* [8]

[7] Albert Feuillerat, *Documents Relating to the Office of the Revels* (Louvain, 1908), p. 469, n. 350.11.

[8] *Ibid.*, p. 471, n. 365.26.

APPENDIX C

No pleasure without some paine

How can the tree but wast, and wither awaie,
That hath not sometyme comfort of the Sonne:
How can that flower but fade, and sone decaie,
That alwaies is with darke clouds ouer ronne.
Is this a life, naie death you maie it call,
That feeles eche paine, and knoweth no ioye at all.

What goodles beast can liue long in good plight,
Or is it life, where sences there be none:
Or what auaileth eyes without their light?
Or els a tonge, to hym that is alone.
Is this a life? naie death you maie it call,
That feeles eche paine, and knowes no ioye at all.

Whereto serue eares, if that there be no sounde,
Or suche a head, where no deuise doeth growe:
But all of plaints, since sorrowe is the grounde,
Whereby the harte doeth pine in deadly woe.
Is this a life, naie death you maie it call,
That feeles eche paine, and knows no ioye at all.

Finis. L. Vaux.

Richard Edwards, *The Paradise of Dainty Devices* (1576-1606), ed. Hyder
E. Rollins (Cambridge, Massachusetts, 1927), p. 72.